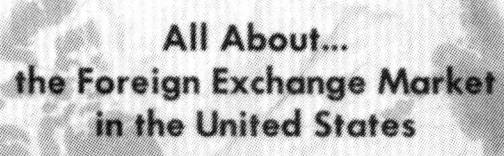

All About...
the Foreign Exchange Market
in the United States

By Sam Y. Cross

Federal Reserve Bank of New York

1998

Books for Business
New York-Hong Kong

All About...
The Foreign Exchange Market
in the United States

by
Sam Y. Cross
The Federal Reserve Bank of New York

ISBN: 0-89499-154-X

Reprinted from the 1998 edition

Books for Business
New York - Hong Kong
http://www.BusinessBooksInternational.com

ALL ABOUT...

─── **CHAPTERS**

———— **C H A P T E R S**

ALL ABOUT...

—— CHAPTERS

ALL ABOUT...

FOREWORD

Over the past forty years, the Federal Reserve Bank of New York has published monographs about the operation of the foreign exchange market in the United States The first of these reports, *The New York Foreign Exchange Market*, by Alan Holmes, was published in 1959 The second, also entitled *The New York Foreign Exchange Market*, was written by Alan Holmes and Francis Schott and published in 1965 The third publication, *Foreign Exchange Markets in the United States*, was written by Roger Kubarych and published in 1978

Each of these publications presents a lucid and informed picture of the foreign exchange market and how it operates, filled with rich insights and reflecting a profound understanding of the market and its complex mechanisms. Roger Kubarych's report, written twenty years ago, provided a valuable analysis of the foreign exchange market that is still read and widely appreciated by persons interested in gaining a deeper understanding of that market.

But the foreign exchange market is always changing, always adapting to a shifting world economy and financial environment. The metamorphosis of the 1980s and '90s in both finance and technology has changed the structure of the market and its operations in profound ways. It is useful to reexamine the foreign exchange market from today's perspective.

The focus of the present book is once again on the U.S. segment of the global foreign exchange market. Chapters 1-3 describe the structure of the market and how it has changed. Chapters 4-6 comment on the main participant groups and the instruments that are traded. Chapters 7-8 look at foreign exchange trading from a micro, rather than macro, point of view—how an individual bank or other dealing firm sees things. Chapters 9-11 comment on some of the broader issues facing the international monetary system and how governments, central banks, and market participants operate within that system. This is followed by an epilogue, emphasizing that there are many unanswered questions, and that we can expect many further changes in the period ahead, changes that we cannot now easily predict.

Markets go back a long time—in English law, the concept was recognized as early as the 11th century—and it is interesting to compare today's foreign exchange market with historical concepts. More than one hundred years ago, Alfred Marshall wrote that "a perfect market is a district, small or large, in which there are many buyers and many sellers, all so keenly on the alert and so well acquainted in one another's affairs that the price of a commodity is always practically the same for the whole of the district."

Today's over-the-counter global market in foreign exchange meets many of the standards that classical economists expected of a smoothly functioning and effective market. There are many buyers and many sellers. Entry by new participants is generally not too difficult. The over-the-counter market is certainly not confined to a single geographical area as the classical standards required. However, with the advance of technology, information is dispersed quickly and efficiently around the globe, with vast amounts of information on political and economic developments affecting exchange rates. As in commodity markets, identical products are being traded in financial centers all around the world. Essentially, the same marks, dollars, francs, and other currencies are being bought and sold, no matter where the purchase takes place. Traders in different centers are continuously in touch and buying and selling from each other. With trading centers open at the same time, there is no evidence of substantial price differences lasting more than momentarily.

Not all features of today's over-the-counter market fully conform to the classical ideals. There is not perfect "transparency," or full and immediate disclosure of all trading activity. Individual traders know about the orders and the flow of trading activity in their own firms, but that information may not be known to everyone else in the market. However, transparency has increased enormously in recent years. With the growth of electronic dealing systems and electronic brokering systems, the price discovery process has become less exclusive and pricing information more broadly disseminated—at least for certain foreign exchange products and currency pairs. Indeed, by most measures, the over-the-counter foreign exchange market is regarded by observers as not only extremely large and liquid, but also efficient and smoothly functioning.

Many persons, both within and outside the Federal Reserve, helped in the preparation of this book, through advice, criticism, and drafting. In the Federal Reserve, first and foremost, before his tragic death, Akbar Akhtar was a close collaborator on the project over an extended period, contributing to all aspects of the effort and helping to produce much of what is here. Dino Kos and his colleagues in the Markets Group were exceedingly helpful. Allan Malz contributed in many important ways. Robin Bensignor, John Kambhu, and Steven Malin also provided much valuable assistance, and Ed Steinberg's contribution as editor was invaluable. At the Federal Reserve Board, Ralph Smith offered very useful suggestions and comments.

Outside of the Federal Reserve, Michael Paulus of Bank of America contributed profoundly and in many ways to the entire project, both in technical matters and on questions of broader philosophy. Christine Kwon also assisted generously. Members of the trading room staff at Morgan Guaranty were also very helpful. At Fuji Bank, staff officials provided valuable assistance. Richard Levich provided very helpful comments.

CHAPTER 1

In a universe with a single currency, there would be no foreign exchange market, no foreign exchange rates, no foreign exchange. But in our world of mainly national currencies, the foreign exchange market plays the indispensable role of providing the essential machinery for making payments across borders, transferring funds and purchasing power from one currency to another, and determining that singularly important price, the exchange rate. Over the past twenty-five years, the way the market has performed those tasks has changed enormously.

1. How The Global Environment Has Changed

Since the early 1970s, with increasing internationalization of financial transactions, the foreign exchange market has been profoundly transformed, not only in size, but in coverage, architecture, and mode of operation. That transformation is the result of structural shifts in the world economy and in the international financial system. Among the major developments that have occurred in the global financial environment are the following:

▶ *A basic change in the international monetary system*, from the fixed exchange rate "par value" requirements of Bretton Woods that existed until the early 1970s to the flexible legal structure of today, in which nations can choose to float their exchange rates or to follow other exchange rate regimes and practices of their choice.

▶ *A tidal wave of financial deregulation throughout the world*, with massive elimination of government controls and restrictions in nearly all countries, resulting in greater freedom for national and international financial transactions, and in greatly increased competition among financial institutions, both within and across national borders.

▶ *A fundamental move toward institutionalization and internationalization of savings and investment*, with funds managers and institutions around the globe having vastly larger sums available, which they are investing and diversifying across borders and currencies in novel ways and in ever larger amounts as they seek to maximize returns.

▶ *A broadening and deepening trend toward international trade liberalization*, within a framework of multilateral trade agreements, such as the Tokyo and the Uruguay Rounds of the General Agreement on Tariffs and Trade, the North American Free Trade Agreement, and U.S. bilateral trade initiatives with China, Japan, and the European Union.

▶ *Major advances in technology,* making possible instantaneous real-time transmission of vast amounts of market information worldwide, immediate and sophisticated manipulation of that information to identify and exploit market opportunities, and rapid and reliable execution of financial transactions—all occurring with a level of efficiency and reduced costs not dreamed possible a generation earlier.

▶ *Breakthroughs in the theory and practice of finance,* resulting not only in the development of innovative new financial instruments and derivative products, but also in advances in thinking that have changed our understanding of the financial system and our techniques for operating within it.

The common theme underlying all of these developments is the role of markets—the growth and development of markets, enhanced freedom and competition in markets, improvements in the efficiency of markets, increased reliance on market forces and mechanisms, and the creation of better market techniques and instruments.

The interplay of these forces, feeding off each other in a dynamic and synergistic way, created a global environment of creativity and ferment. In the 1970s, exchange rates became more volatile and imbalances in international payments grew much larger for well-known reasons: the advent of a floating exchange rate system, deregulation, and major macroeconomic shifts in the world economy. That caused financing needs to expand, which—at a time of rapid technological advance—provided fertile ground for the development of new financial products and mechanisms. These innovations helped market participants circumvent existing controls and encouraged further moves toward deregulation, which led to additional new products, facilitated the financing of still larger imbalances, and encouraged a trend toward institutionalization of savings and diversification of investment. Financial markets grew progressively larger and more sophisticated, integrated, and efficient.

In that environment, foreign exchange trading increased rapidly and changed intrinsically. The market has expanded from one of banks to one in which many other kinds of financial and non-financial institutions also participate—including nonfinancial corporations, investment firms, pension funds, and hedge funds. Its focus has broadened from servicing importers and exporters to handling the vast amounts of overseas investment and other capital flows that currently take place. It has evolved from a series of loosely connected national financial centers to a single integrated international market that plays a far more extensive and direct role in our economies, affecting all aspects of our lives and our prosperity.

2. How Foreign Exchange Turnover Has Grown

In 1998, the Federal Reserve's most recently published survey of reporting dealers in the United States estimated that foreign exchange turnover in the U.S. market was $351 billion a day, after adjustments for double counting. That total is an increase of 43% above the estimated turnover in 1995 and more than 60 times the turnover in 1977, the first year for which roughly comparable survey data are available.

In some ways, this estimate understates the growth and the present size of the U.S. foreign exchange market. The $351 billion estimated daily turnover covered only the three *traditional* instruments in the "over-the-counter" (OTC) market—*spot*, *outright forwards*, and *foreign exchange (FX) swaps*; it did not include *over-the-counter currency options* and *currency swaps* traded in the OTC market, which totaled about $32 billion a day in notional value (or face value) in 1998. Nor did it include the two products traded, not "over-the-counter," but in organized exchanges— *currency futures* and *exchange-traded currency options*, for which the notional value of the turnover was perhaps $10 billion per day.[1]

The global foreign exchange market also has shown phenomenal growth. In 1998, in a survey under the auspices of the Bank for International Settlements (BIS), global turnover of reporting dealers was estimated at about $1.49 trillion per day for the traditional products, plus an additional $97 billion for *over-the-counter* currency options and currency swaps, and a further $12 billion for currency instruments traded on the organized exchanges. In the traditional products, global foreign exchange turnover, measured in current exchange rates, increased by more than 80 percent between 1992 and 1998.

The expansion in foreign exchange turnover, in the United States and globally, reflects the continuing growth of international trade and the prodigious expansion in global finance and investment during recent years. With respect to trade, the dollar value of United States international transactions in goods and services—the sum of exports and imports— tripled between 1980 and 1995 to around 15 times its 1970 level. International trade in the global economy also has expanded at a rapid pace. World merchandise trade is now more than 2½ times its 1980 level (Figure 1-1).

FIGURE 1-1

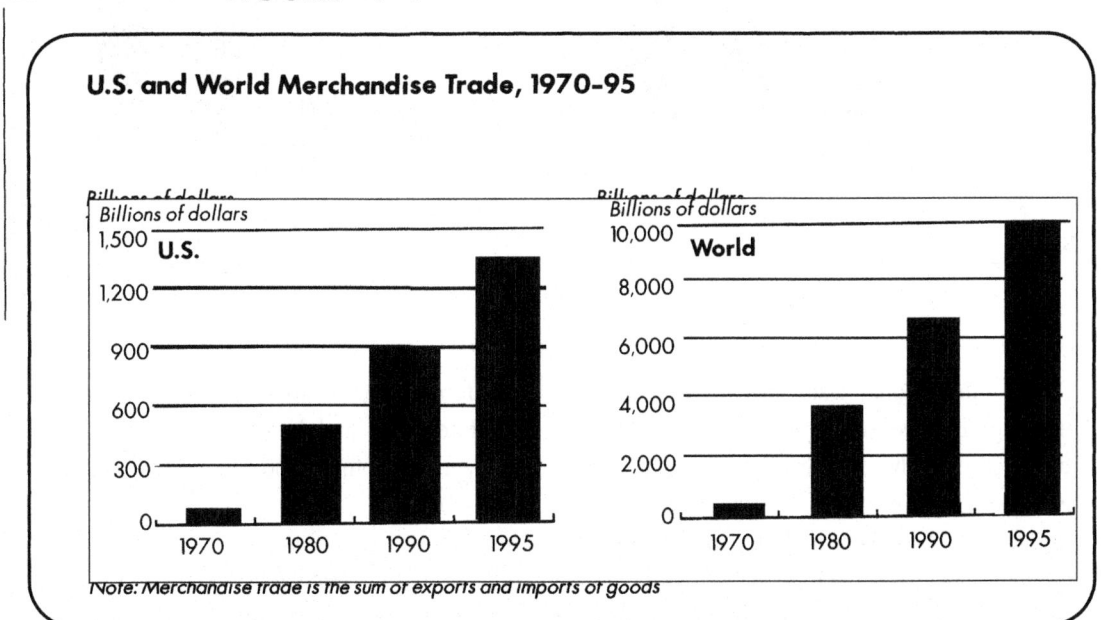

U.S. and World Merchandise Trade, 1970-95

Note: Merchandise trade is the sum of exports and imports of goods

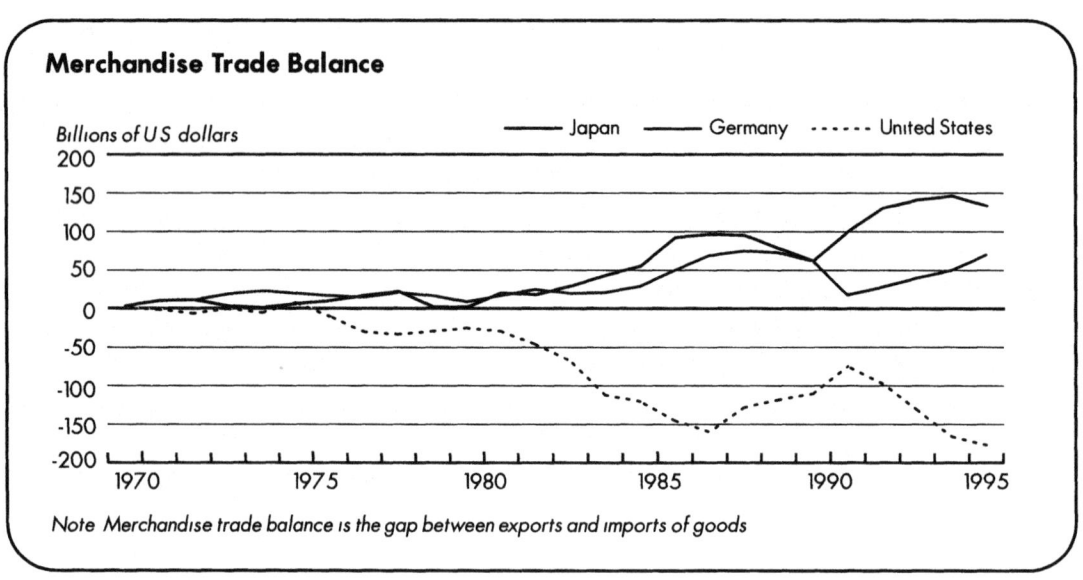

Merchandise Trade Balance

Billions of US dollars — Japan — Germany ----- United States

Note Merchandise trade balance is the gap between exports and imports of goods

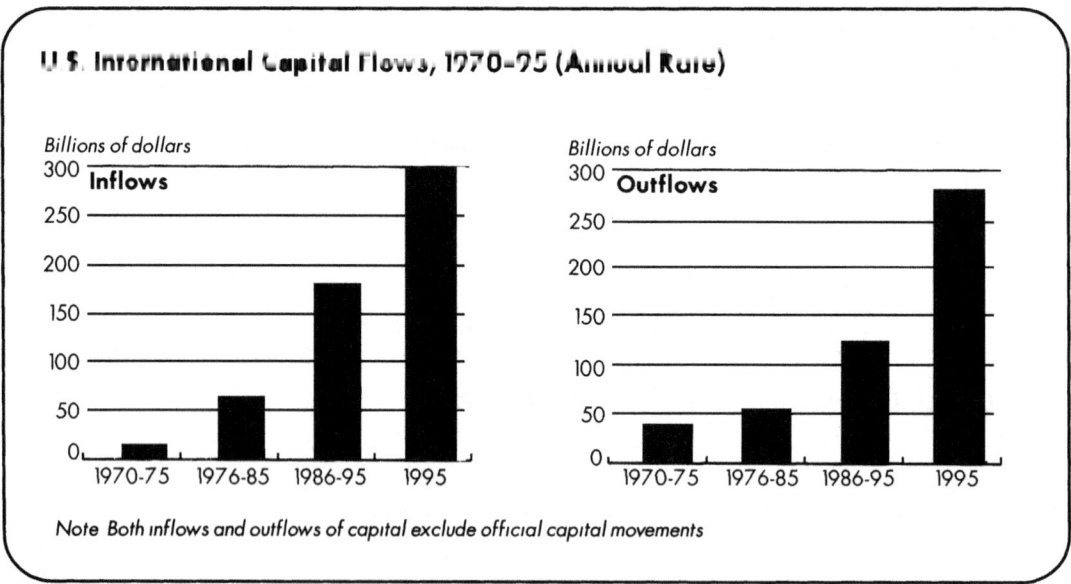

U.S. International Capital Flows, 1970-95 (Annual Rate)

Billions of dollars — Inflows

Billions of dollars — Outflows

Note Both inflows and outflows of capital exclude official capital movements

But international trade cannot account for the huge increase in the U.S. foreign exchange turnover over the past twenty-five years. The enormous expansion of international capital transactions, both here and abroad, has been a dominant force. U.S. international capital inflows, including sales of U.S. bonds and equities to foreigners, acquisition of U.S. factories by foreigners, and bank deposit inflows, have averaged more than $180 billion per year since the mid-80s.

Large and persistent external trade and payments deficits in the United States and

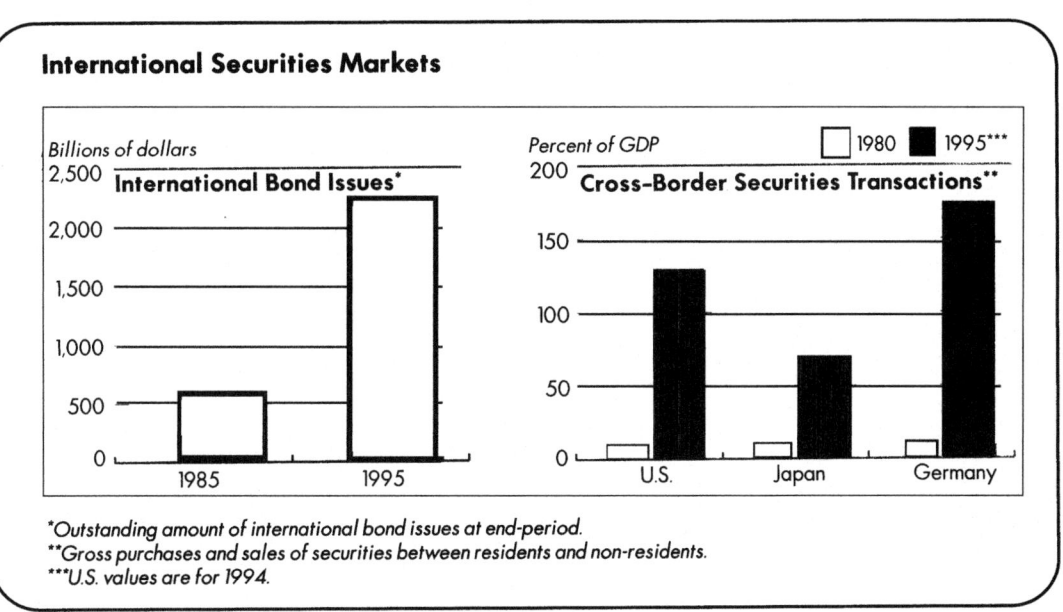

International Securities Markets

Billions of dollars

International Bond Issues*

Percent of GDP   ☐ 1980 ■ 1995***

Cross-Border Securities Transactions**

1985   1995

U.S.   Japan   Germany

*Outstanding amount of international bond issues at end-period.
**Gross purchases and sales of securities between residents and non-residents.
***U.S. values are for 1994.

corresponding surpluses abroad have contributed to the growth in financing. Through much of the period since 1983, the United States has recorded trade deficits in the range of $100-$200 billion per year, while Japan and, to a lesser extent, Germany have registered substantial trade surpluses. In contrast, all three countries experienced only modest trade deficits or surpluses through the 1960s and early 1970s.

The internationalization of financial activity has increased rapidly. Cross-border bank claims are now nearly five times the level of 15 years ago; as a percentage of the combined GDP of the OECD countries, these claims have risen from about 25 percent in 1980 to about 42

percent in 1995. During that same period, cross-border securities transactions in the three largest economies—United States, Japan, and Germany—expanded from less than 10 percent of GDP to around 70 percent of GDP in Japan and to well above 100 percent of GDP in Germany and the United States (Figure 1-2). Annual issuance of international bonds has more than quadrupled during the past ten years (Figure 1-2). Between 1988 and 1993, securities settlements through Euroclear and Cedel—the two main Euro market clearing houses—increased six-fold.

All of this provided fertile ground for growth in foreign exchange trading.

CHAPTER 2

1. Why We Need Foreign Exchange

Almost every nation has its own *national currency* or monetary unit—its dollar, its peso, its rupee—used for making and receiving payments within its own borders. But foreign currencies are usually needed for payments across national borders. Thus, in any nation whose residents conduct business abroad or engage in financial transactions with persons in other countries, there must be a mechanism for providing access to foreign currencies, so that payments can be made in a form acceptable to foreigners. In other words, there is need for "foreign exchange" transactions—exchanges of one currency for another.

2. What " Foreign Exchange " Means

"Foreign exchange" refers to money denominated in the currency of another nation or group of nations. Any person who exchanges money denominated in *his own* nation's currency for money denominated in *another* nation's currency acquires foreign exchange. That holds true whether the *amount* of the transaction is equal to a few dollars or to billions of dollars; whether the *person involved* is a tourist cashing a traveler's check in a restaurant abroad or an investor exchanging hundreds of millions of dollars for the acquisition of a foreign company; and whether the *form of money* being acquired is foreign currency notes, foreign currency-denominated bank deposits, or other short-term claims denominated in foreign currency. A foreign exchange transaction is still a shift of funds, or short-term financial claims, from one country and currency to another.

Thus, within the United States, any money denominated in any currency other than the U.S. dollar is, broadly speaking, "foreign exchange."

Foreign exchange can be cash, funds available on credit cards and debit cards, traveler's checks, bank deposits, or other short-term claims. It is still "foreign exchange" if it is a short-term negotiable financial claim denominated in a currency other than the U.S. dollar.

But, in the foreign exchange market described in this book—the international network of major foreign exchange dealers engaged in high-volume trading around the world—foreign exchange transactions almost always take the form of an exchange of *bank deposits* of different national currency denominations. If one bank agrees to sell dollars for Deutsche marks to another bank, there will be an exchange between the two parties of a dollar bank deposit for a DEM bank deposit. In this book, "foreign exchange" means a *bank balance denominated in a foreign (non-U.S. dollar) currency.*

3. Role Of The Exchange Rate

The exchange rate is a *price*—the number of units of one nation's currency that must be surrendered in order to acquire one unit of another nation's currency. There are scores of "exchange rates" for the U.S. dollar. In the spot market, there is an exchange rate for every other national currency

traded in that market, as well as for various composite currencies or constructed monetary units such as the International Monetary Fund's "SDR," the European Monetary Union's "ECU," and beginning in 1999, the "euro." There are also various "trade-weighted" or "effective" rates designed to show a currency's movements against an average of various other currencies (see Box 2-1). Quite apart from the spot rates, there are additional exchange rates for other delivery dates, in the forward markets. Accordingly, although we talk about the dollar exchange rate in

the market, and it is useful to do so, there is no single, or unique dollar exchange rate in the market, just as there is no unique dollar interest rate in the market.

A market price is determined by the inter-action of buyers and sellers in that market, and a market exchange rate between two currencies is determined by the interaction of the official and private participants in the foreign exchange rate market. For a currency with an exchange rate that is fixed, or set by the monetary authorities, the central bank or another official body is a key participant in the market, standing ready to buy or sell the currency as necessary to maintain the authorized pegged rate or range. But in the United States, where the authorities do not intervene in the foreign exchange market on a continuous basis to influence the exchange rate, market participation is made up of individuals, nonfinancial firms, banks, official bodies, and other private institutions from all over the world that are buying and selling dollars at that particular time.

The participants in the foreign exchange market are thus a heterogeneous group. Some of the buyers and sellers may be involved in the "goods" market, conducting international transactions for the purchase or sale of merchandise. Some may be engaged in "direct investment" in plant and equipment, or in "portfolio investment," dealing across borders in stocks and bonds and other financial assets, while others may be in the "money market," trading short-term debt instruments internationally. The various investors, hedgers, and speculators may be focused on any time period, from a few minutes to several years. But, whether official or private, and whether their motive be investing, hedging, speculating, arbitraging, paying for imports, or seeking to influence the rate, they are all part of the aggregate demand for and supply

BOX 2-1

BILATERAL AND TRADE-WEIGHTED EXCHANGE RATES

Market trading is bilateral, and spot and forward market exchange rates are quoted in bilateral terms—the dollar versus the pound, franc, or peso. Changes in the dollar's average value on a multilateral basis—(i.e., its value against a group or basket of currencies) are measured by using various statistical indexes that have been constructed to capture the dollar's movements on a trade-weighted average, or effective exchange rate basis. Among others, the staff of the Federal Reserve Board of Governors has developed and regularly publishes such indexes, which measure the average value of the dollar against the currencies of both a narrow group and a broad group of other countries. Such trade-weighted and other indexes are not traded in the OTC spot or forward markets, where only the constituent currencies are traded. However, it is possible to buy and sell certain dollar index based futures and exchange-traded options in the exchange-traded market.

of the currencies involved, and they all play a role in determining the market exchange rate at that instant.

Given the diverse views, interests, and time frames of the participants, predicting the future course of exchange rates is a particularly complex and uncertain business. At the same time, since the exchange rate influences such a vast array of participants and business decisions, it is a pervasive and singularly important price in an open economy, influencing consumer prices, investment decisions, interest rates, economic growth, the location of industry, and much else. The role of the foreign exchange market in the determination of that price is critically important.

4. Payment And Settlement Systems

Just as each nation has its own national currency, so also does each nation have its own payment and settlement system—that is, its own set of institutions and legally acceptable arrangements for making payments and executing financial transactions within that country, using its national currency. "Payment" is the transmission of an *instruction* to transfer value that results from a transaction in the economy, and "settlement" is the final and unconditional *transfer* of the value specified in a payment instruction. Thus, if a customer pays a department store bill by check, "payment" occurs when the check is placed in the hands of the department store, and "settlement" occurs when the check clears and the department store's bank account is credited. If the customer pays the bill with cash, payment and settlement are simultaneous.

When two traders enter a deal and agree to undertake a foreign exchange transaction, they are agreeing on the *terms* of a currency exchange and committing the resources of their respective institutions to that agreement. But the *execution* of that exchange—the settlement—does not take place until later.

Executing a foreign exchange transaction requires two transfers of money value, in opposite directions, since it involves the exchange of one national currency for another. Execution of the transaction engages the payment and settlement systems of both nations, and those systems play a key role in the operations of the foreign exchange market.

Payment systems have evolved and grown more sophisticated over time. At present, various forms of payment are legally acceptable in the United States—payments can be made, for example, by cash, check, automated clearinghouse (a mechanism developed as a substitute for certain forms of paper payments), and electronic funds transfer (for large value transfers between banks). Each of these accepted forms of payment has its own settlement techniques and arrangements.

By number of transactions, most payments in the United States are still made with cash (currency and coin) or checks. However, the electronic funds transfer systems, which account for less than 0.1 percent of the *number* of all payments transactions in the United States, account for more than 80 percent of the value of payments. Thus,

BOX 2-2

PAYMENTS VIA FEDWIRE AND CHIPS

When a payment is executed over Fedwire, a regional Federal Reserve Bank debits on its books the account of the sending bank and credits the account of the receiving bank, so that there is an immediate transfer from the sending bank and delivery to the receiving bank of "central bank money" (i.e., a deposit claim on that Federal Reserve Bank). A Fedwire payment is "settled" when the receiving bank has its deposit account at the Fed credited with the funds or is notified of the payment. Fedwire is a "real-time gross settlements" (or RTGS) system. To control risk on Fedwire, the Federal Reserve imposes charges on participants for intra-day (daylight) overdrafts beyond a permissible allowance.

In contrast to Fedwire, payments processed over CHIPS are finally "settled," not individually during the course of the day, but collectively at the end of the business day, after the net debit or credit position of each CHIPS participant (against all other CHIPS participants) has been determined. Final settlement of CHIPS obligations occurs by Fedwire transfer (delivery of "central bank money"). Settlement is initiated when those CHIPS participants in a net debit position for the day's CHIPS activity pay their day's obligations. If a commercial bank that is scheduled to receive CHIPS payments makes funds available to its customers before CHIPS settlement occurs at the end of the day, that commercial bank is exposed to some risk of loss if CHIPS settlement cannot occur. To ensure that settlement does, in fact, occur, the New York Clearing House has put in place a system of net debit caps and a loss-sharing arrangement backed up by collateral as a risk control mechanism.

electronic funds transfer systems represent a key and indispensable component of the payment and settlement systems. It is the electronic funds transfer systems that execute the inter-bank transfers between dealers in the foreign exchange market. The two electronic funds transfer systems operating in the United States are CHIPS (Clearing House Interbank Payments System), a privately owned system run by the New York Clearing House, and Fedwire, a system run by the Federal Reserve (see Box 2-2).

Other countries also have large-value interbank funds transfer systems, similar to Fedwire and CHIPS in the United States. In the United Kingdom, the pound sterling leg of a foreign exchange transaction is likely to be settled through CHAPS—the Clearing House Association Payments System, an RTGS system whose member banks settle with each other through their accounts at the Bank of England. In Germany, the Deutsche mark leg of a transaction is settled through EAF—an electronic payments system where settlements are made through accounts at Germany's central bank, the Deutsche Bundesbank. A new payment system, named Target, has been designed to link RTGS systems within the European Community, to enable participants to handle transactions in the euro upon its introduction on January 1, 1999.

Globally, more than 80 percent of global foreign exchange transactions have a dollar leg. Thus, the amount of daily dollar settlements is huge, one trillion dollars per day or more. The settlement of foreign exchange transactions accounts for the bulk of total dollar payments processed through CHIPS each day.

The matter of settlement practices is of particular importance to the foreign exchange

market because of "settlement risk," the risk that one party to a foreign exchange transaction will pay out the currency it is selling but not receive the currency it is buying. Because of time zone differences and delays caused by the banks' own internal procedures and corresponding banking arrangements, a substantial amount of time can pass between a payment and the time the counter-payment is received—and a substantial credit risk can arise. Efforts to reduce or eliminate settlement risk are discussed in Chapter 8.

--- CHAPTER 3

1. It Is The World's Largest Market

The foreign exchange market is by far the largest and most liquid market in the world. The estimated worldwide turnover of reporting dealers, at around $1½ trillion a day, is several times the level of turnover in the U.S. Government securities market, the world's second largest market. Turnover is equivalent to more than $200 in foreign exchange market transactions, every business day of the year, for every man, woman, and child on earth!

The breadth, depth, and liquidity of the market are truly impressive. Individual trades of $200 million to $500 million are not uncommon. Quoted prices change as often as 20 times a minute. It has been estimated that the world's most active exchange rates can change up to 18,000 times during a single day.[2] Large trades can be made, yet econometric studies indicate that prices tend to move in relatively small increments, a sign of a smoothly functioning and liquid market.

While turnover of around $1½ trillion per day is a good indication of the level of activity and liquidity in the global foreign exchange market, it is not necessarily a useful measure of other forces in the world economy. Almost two-thirds of the total represents transactions among the reporting dealers themselves—with only one-third accounted for by their transactions with financial and non-financial customers. It is important to realize that an initial dealer transaction with a customer in the foreign exchange market often leads to multiple further transactions, sometimes over an extended period, as the dealer institutions readjust their own positions to hedge, manage, or offset the risks involved. The result is that the amount of trading with customers of a large dealer institution active

in the interbank market often accounts for a very small share of that institution's total foreign exchange activity.

Among the various financial centers around the world, the largest amount of foreign exchange trading takes place in the United Kingdom, even though that nation's currency—the pound sterling—is less widely traded in the market than several others. As shown in Figure 3-1, the United Kingdom accounts for about 32 percent of the global total; the United States ranks a distant second with about 18 percent, and Japan is third with 8 percent. Thus, together, the three largest markets—one each in the European, Western Hemisphere, and Asian time zones—account for about 58 percent of global trading. After these three leaders comes Singapore with 7 percent.

--- FIGURE 3-1

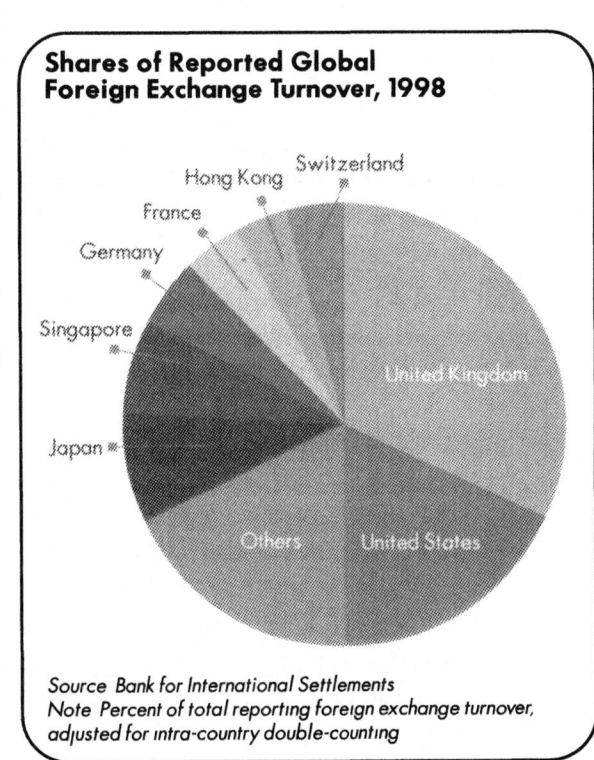

Shares of Reported Global Foreign Exchange Turnover, 1998

Source Bank for International Settlements
Note Percent of total reporting foreign exchange turnover, adjusted for intra-country double-counting

The large volume of trading activity in the United Kingdom reflects London's strong position as an international financial center where a large number of financial institutions are located. In the 1998 foreign exchange market turnover survey, 213 foreign exchange dealer institutions in the United Kingdom reported trading activity to the Bank of England, compared with 93 in the United States reporting to the Federal Reserve Bank of New York.

In foreign exchange trading, London benefits not only from its proximity to major Eurocurrency credit markets and other financial markets, but also from its geographical location and time zone. In addition to being open when the numerous other financial centers in Europe are open, London's morning hours overlap with the late hours in a number of Asian and Middle East markets; London's afternoon sessions correspond to the morning periods in the large North American market. Thus, surveys have indicated that there is more foreign exchange trading in dollars in London than in the United States, and more foreign exchange trading in marks than in Germany. However, the bulk of trading in London, about 85 percent, is accounted for by foreign-owned (non-U.K. owned) institutions, with U.K.-based dealers of North American institutions reporting 49 percent, or three times the share of U.K.-owned institutions there.

2. It Is A Twenty-Four Hour Market

During the past quarter century, the concept of a twenty-four hour market has become a reality. Somewhere on the planet, financial centers are open for business, and banks and other institutions are trading the dollar and other currencies, every hour of the day and night, aside from possible minor gaps on weekends. In financial centers around the world, business hours overlap; as some centers close, others open and begin to trade. The foreign exchange market follows the sun around the earth.

The international date line is located in the western Pacific, and each business day arrives first in the Asia-Pacific financial centers— first Wellington, New Zealand, then Sydney, Australia, followed by Tokyo, Hong Kong, and Singapore. A few hours later, while markets remain active in those Asian centers, trading begins in Bahrain and elsewhere in the Middle East. Later still, when it is late in the business day in Tokyo, markets in Europe open for business. Subsequently, when it is early afternoon in Europe, trading in New York and other U.S. centers starts. Finally, completing the circle, when it is mid- or late-afternoon in the United States, the next day has arrived in the Asia-Pacific area, the first markets there have opened, and the process begins again.

The twenty-four hour market means that exchange rates and market conditions can change at any time in response to developments that can take place at any time. It also means that traders and other market participants must be alert to the possibility that a sharp move in an exchange rate can occur during an off hour, elsewhere in the world. The large dealing institutions have adapted to these conditions, and have introduced various arrangements for monitoring markets and trading on a twenty-four hour basis. Some keep their New York or other trading desks open

FIGURE 3-2

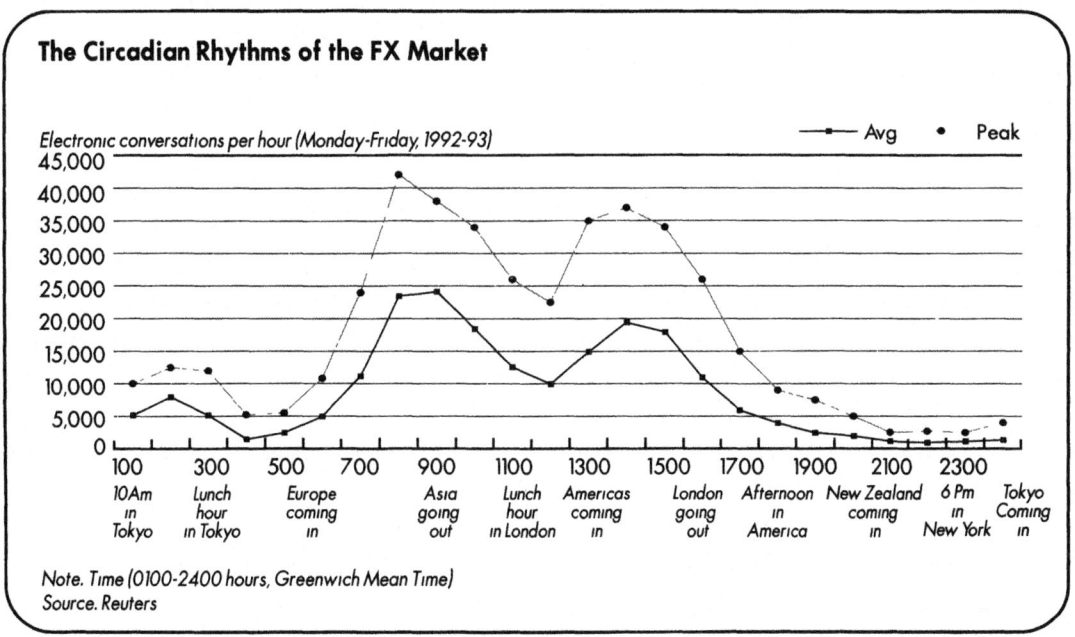

The Circadian Rhythms of the FX Market

Electronic conversations per hour (Monday-Friday, 1992-93)

Legend: —■— Avg   • Peak

Note. Time (0100-2400 hours, Greenwich Mean Time)
Source. Reuters

twenty-four hours a day, others pass the torch from one office to the next, and still others follow different approaches.

However, foreign exchange activity does not flow evenly. Over the course of a day, there is a cycle characterized by periods of very heavy activity and other periods of relatively light activity. Most of the trading takes place when the largest number of potential counterparties is available or accessible *on a global basis.* (Figure 3-2 gives a general sense of participation levels in the global foreign exchange market by tracking electronic conversations per hour.) Market liquidity is of great importance to participants. Sellers want to sell when they have access to the maximum number of potential buyers, and buyers want to buy when they have access to the maximum number of potential sellers.

Business is heavy when both the U.S. markets and the major European markets are open—that is, when it is morning in New York and afternoon in London. In the New York market, nearly two-thirds of the day's activity typically takes place in the morning hours. Activity normally becomes very slow in New York in the mid- to late afternoon, after European markets have closed and before the Tokyo, Hong Kong, and Singapore markets have opened.

Given this uneven flow of business around the clock, market participants often will respond less aggressively to an exchange rate development that occurs at a relatively inactive time of day, and will wait to see whether the development is confirmed when the major markets open. Some institutions pay little attention to developments in less active markets. Nonetheless, the twenty-four hour market does provide a continuous "real-time" market assessment of the ebb and flow of influences and attitudes with respect to the traded currencies, and an opportunity for a quick judgment of unexpected events. With many traders carrying pocket monitors, it has become relatively easy to stay in touch with market developments at all times—indeed, too easy, some harassed traders might say. The foreign exchange market provides a kind of never-ending beauty contest or horse race, where market participants can continuously adjust their bets to reflect their changing views.

---

3. The Market Is Made Up Of An International Network Dealers

The market consists of a limited number of major dealer institutions that are particularly active in foreign exchange, trading with customers and (more often) with each other. Most, but not all, are commercial banks and investment banks. These dealer institutions are geographically dispersed, located in numerous financial centers around the world. Wherever located, these institutions are linked to, and in close communication with, each other through telephones, computers, and other electronic means.

There are around 2,000 dealer institutions whose foreign exchange activities are covered by the Bank for International Settlements' central bank survey, and who, essentially, make up the global foreign exchange market. A much smaller sub-set of those institutions account for the bulk of trading and market-making activity. It is estimated that there are 100-200 market-making banks worldwide; major players are fewer than that.

At a time when there is much talk about an integrated world economy and "the global village," the foreign exchange market comes closest to functioning in a truly global fashion, linking the various foreign exchange trading centers from around the world into a single, unified, cohesive, worldwide market. Foreign exchange trading takes place among dealers and other market professionals in a large number of individual financial centers— New York, Chicago, Los Angeles, London, Tokyo, Singapore, Frankfurt, Paris, Zurich, Milan, and many, many others. But no matter in which financial center a trade occurs, the same currencies, or rather, bank deposits denominated in the same currencies, are being bought and sold.

A foreign exchange dealer buying dollars in one of those markets actually is buying a dollar-denominated deposit in a bank located in the United States, or a claim of a bank abroad on a dollar deposit in a bank located in the United States. This holds true regardless of the location of the financial center at which the dollar deposit is purchased. Similarly, a dealer buying Deutsche marks, no matter where the purchase is made, actually is buying a mark deposit in a bank in Germany or a claim on a mark deposit in a bank in Germany. And so on for other currencies.

Each nation's market has its own infrastructure. For foreign exchange market operations as well as for other matters, each country enforces its own laws, banking regulations, accounting rules, and tax code, and, as noted above, it operates its own payment and settlement systems. Thus, even in a global foreign exchange market with currencies traded on essentially the same terms simultaneously in many financial centers, there are different national financial systems and infrastructures through which transactions are executed, and within which currencies are held.

With access to all of the foreign exchange markets generally open to participants from all countries, and with vast amounts of market information transmitted simultaneously and almost instantly to dealers throughout the world, there is an enormous amount of cross-border foreign exchange trading among dealers as well as between dealers and their customers. At any moment, the exchange rates of major currencies tend to be virtually identical in all of the financial centers where there is active trading. Rarely are there such substantial price differences among major centers as to provide major opportunities for arbitrage. In pricing, the various financial centers that are open for business and active at any one time are effectively integrated into a single market.

Accordingly, a bank in the United States is likely to trade foreign exchange at least as frequently with banks in London, Frankfurt, and other open foreign centers as with other banks in the United States. Surveys indicate that when major dealing institutions in the United States trade with other dealers, 58 percent of the transactions are with dealers located outside the United States. The United States is not unique in that respect. Dealer institutions in other major countries also report that more than half of their trades are with dealers that are across borders; dealers also use brokers located both domestically and abroad.

4. The Market's Most Widely Traded Currency Is The Dollar

The dollar is by far the most widely traded currency. According to the 1998 survey, the dollar was one of the two currencies involved in an estimated 87 percent of global foreign exchange transactions, equal to about $1.3 trillion a day. In part, the widespread use of the dollar reflects its substantial international role as: "investment" currency in many capital markets, "reserve" currency held by many central banks, "transaction" currency in many international commodity markets, "invoice" currency in many contracts, and "intervention" currency employed by monetary authorities in market operations to influence their own exchange rates.

In addition, the widespread trading of the dollar reflects its use as a "vehicle" currency in foreign exchange transactions, a use that reinforces, and is reinforced by, its international role in trade and finance. For most pairs of currencies, the market practice is to trade each of the two currencies against a common third currency as a vehicle, rather than to trade the two currencies directly against each other. The

vehicle currency used most often is the dollar, although by the mid-1990s the Deutsche mark also had become an important vehicle, with its use, especially in Europe, having increased sharply during the 1980s and '90s.

Thus, a trader wanting to shift funds from one currency to another, say, from Swedish krona to Philippine pesos, will probably sell krona for U.S. dollars and then sell the U.S. dollars for pesos. Although this approach results in two transactions rather than one, it may be the preferred way, since the dollar/Swedish krona market, and the dollar/Philippine peso market are much more active and liquid and have much better information than a bilateral market for the two currencies directly against each other. By using the dollar or some other currency as a vehicle, banks and other foreign exchange market participants can limit more of their working balances to the vehicle currency, rather than holding and managing many currencies, and can concentrate their research and information sources on the vehicle.

Use of a vehicle currency greatly reduces the number of exchange rates that must be dealt with in a multilateral system. In a system of 10 currencies, if one currency is selected as vehicle currency and used for all transactions, there would be a total of *nine* currency pairs or exchange rates to be dealt with (i.e., one exchange rate for the vehicle currency against each of the others), whereas if no vehicle currency were used, there would be *45* exchange rates to be dealt with. In a system of 100 currencies with no vehicle currencies, potentially there would be 4,950 currency pairs or exchange rates [the formula is: $n(n-1)/2$]. Thus, using a vehicle currency can yield the advantages of fewer, larger, and more liquid markets with fewer currency balances, reduced informational needs, and simpler operations.

The U.S. dollar took on a major vehicle currency role with the introduction of the Bretton Woods par value system, in which most nations met their IMF exchange rate obligations by buying and selling U.S. dollars to maintain a par value relationship for their own currency against the U.S. dollar. The dollar was a convenient vehicle, not only because of its central role in the exchange rate system and its widespread use as a reserve currency, but also because of the presence of large and liquid dollar money and other financial markets, and, in time, the Euro-dollar markets where dollars needed for (or resulting from) foreign exchange transactions could conveniently be borrowed (or placed).

Changing conditions in the 1980s and 1990s altered this situation. In particular, the Deutsche mark began to play a much more significant role as a vehicle currency and, more importantly, in direct "cross trading."

As the European Community moved toward economic integration and monetary unification, the relationship of the European Monetary System (EMS) currencies to each other became of greater concern than the relationship of their currencies to the dollar. An intra-European currency market developed, centering on the mark and on Germany as the strongest currency and largest economy. Direct intervention in members' currencies, rather than through the dollar, became widely practiced. Events such as the EMS currency crisis of September 1992, when a number of European currencies came under severe market pressure against the mark, confirmed the extent to which direct use of the DEM for intervening in the exchange market could be more effective than going through the dollar.

Against this background, there was very rapid growth in *direct cross rate trading* involving the Deutsche mark, much of it against European currencies, during the 1980s and '90s. (A "cross rate" is an exchange rate between two *non-dollar* currencies—e.g., DEM/Swiss franc, DEM/pound, and DEM/yen.) As discussed in Chapter 5, there are *derived* cross rates calculated from the dollar rates of each of the two currencies, and there are *direct* cross rates that come from *direct trading* between the two currencies—which can result in narrower spreads where there is a viable market. In a number of European countries, the volume of trading of the local currency against the Deutsche mark grew to exceed local currency trading against the dollar, and the practice developed of using cross rates between the DEM and other European currencies to determine the dollar rates for those currencies.

With its increased use as a vehicle currency and its role in cross trading, the Deutsche mark was involved in 30 percent of global currency turnover in the 1998 survey. That was still far below the dollar (which was involved in 87 percent of global turnover), but well above the Japanese yen (ranked third, at 21 percent), and the pound sterling (ranked fourth, at 11 percent).

5. It Is An " Over The - Counter " Market With An " Exchange -Traded " Segment

Until the 1970s, all foreign exchange trading in the United States (and elsewhere) was handled "over-the-counter," (OTC) by banks in different locations making deals via telephone and telex. In the United States, the OTC market was then, and is now, largely unregulated *as a market*. Buying and selling foreign currencies is considered the exercise of an express banking power. Thus, a commercial bank in the United States does not need any special authorization to trade or deal in foreign exchange. Similarly, securities firms and brokerage firms do not need permission from the Securities and Exchange Commission (SEC) or any other body to engage in foreign exchange activity. Transactions can be carried out on whatever terms and with whatever provisions are permitted by law and acceptable to the two counterparties, subject to the standard commercial law governing business transactions in the United States.

There are no official rules or restrictions in the United States governing the hours or conditions of trading. The trading conventions have been developed mostly by market participants. There is no official code prescribing what constitutes good market practice. However, the Foreign Exchange Committee, an independent body sponsored by the Federal Reserve Bank of New York and composed of representatives from institutions participating in the market, produces and regularly updates its report on *Guidelines for Foreign Exchange Trading*. These *Guidelines* seek to clarify common market practices and offer "best practice recommendations" with respect to trading activities, relationships, and other matters. The report is a purely advisory document designed to foster the healthy functioning and development of the foreign exchange market in the United States.

Although the OTC market is not regulated as a market in the way that the organized exchanges are regulated, regulatory authorities examine the foreign exchange market activities of banks and certain other institutions participating in the OTC market. As with other business activities in which these institutions are engaged, examiners look at trading systems, activities, and exposure, focusing on the safety and soundness of the institution and its activities. Examinations deal with such matters as capital adequacy, control systems, disclosure, sound banking practice, legal compliance, and other factors relating to the safety and soundness of the institution.

The OTC market accounts for well over 90 percent of total U.S. foreign exchange market activity, covering both the traditional (pre-1970) products (*spot, outright forwards*, and *FX swaps*) as well as the more recently introduced (post-1970) OTC products (*currency options* and *currency swaps*). On the "organized exchanges," foreign exchange products traded are *currency futures* and certain *currency options*.

Trading practices on the organized exchanges, and the regulatory arrangements covering the exchanges, are markedly different from those in the OTC market. In the exchanges, trading takes place publicly in a centralized location. Hours, trading practices, and other matters are regulated by the particular exchange; products are standardized. There are margin payments, daily marking to market, and cash settlements through a central clearinghouse. With respect to regulation, exchanges at which currency *futures* are traded are under the jurisdiction of the Commodity Futures Trading Corporation (CFTC); in the case of currency *options*, either the CFTC or the Securities and Exchange Commission serves as regulator, depending on whether securities are traded on the exchange.

Steps are being taken internationally to help improve the risk management practices of dealers in the foreign exchange market, and to encourage greater transparency and disclosure. With respect to the internationally active banks, there has been a move under the auspices of the Basle Committee on Banking Supervision of the BIS to introduce greater consistency internationally to risk-based capital adequacy requirements. Over the past decade, the regulators of a number of nations have accepted common rules proposed by the Basle Committee with respect to capital adequacy requirements for *credit* risk, covering exposures of internationally active banks in all activities, including foreign exchange. Further proposals of the Basle Committee for risk-based capital requirements for *market* risk have been adopted more recently. With respect to investment firms and other financial institutions, international discussions have not yet produced agreements on common capital adequacy standards.

CHAPTER 4

1. Foreign Exchange Dealers

Most commercial banks in the United States customarily have bought and sold foreign exchange for their customers as one of their standard financial services. But beginning at a very early stage in the development of the over-the-counter market, a small number of large commercial banks operating in New York and other U.S. money centers took on foreign exchange trading as a major business activity. They operated for corporate and other customers, serving as intermediaries and market makers. In this capacity, they transacted business as correspondents for many other commercial banks throughout the country, while also buying and selling foreign exchange for their own accounts. These major dealer banks found it useful to trade with each other frequently, as they sought to find buyers and sellers and to manage their positions. This group developed into an *interbank* market for foreign exchange.

While these commercial banks continue to play a dominant role, being a major dealer in the foreign exchange market has ceased to be their exclusive domain. During the past 25 years, some investment banking firms and other financial institutions have become emulators and direct competitors of the commercial banks as dealers in the over-the-counter market. They now also serve as major dealers, executing transactions that previously would have been handled only by the large commercial banks, and providing foreign exchange services to a variety of customers in competition with the dealer banks. They are now part of the network of foreign exchange dealers that constitutes the U.S. segment of the foreign exchange market. Although it is still called the "interbank" market in foreign exchange, it is more accurately an "interdealer" market.

The 1998 foreign exchange market turnover survey by the Federal Reserve Bank of New York covered the operations of the 93 major foreign exchange dealers in the United States. The total volume of transactions of the reporting dealers, corrected for double-counting among themselves, at $351 billion per day in traditional products, plus $32 billion in currency options and currency swaps, represents the estimated total turnover in the U.S. over-the-counter market in 1998.

To be included in the reporting dealers group surveyed by the Federal Reserve, an institution must be located in the United States and play an active role as a dealer in the market. There are no formal requirements for inclusion, other than having a high enough level of foreign exchange trading activity. Of course, an institution must have a name that is known and accepted to enable it to obtain from other participants the credit lines essential to active participation.

Of the 93 reporting dealers in 1998, 82 were commercial banks, and 11 were investment banks or insurance firms. All of the large U.S. money center banks are active dealers. Most of the 93 institutions are located in New York, but a number of them are based in Boston, Chicago, San Francisco, and other U.S. financial centers. Many of the dealer institutions have outlets in other countries as well as in the United States.

Included in the group are a substantial number of U.S. branches and subsidiaries of major foreign banks—banks from Japan, the United Kingdom, Germany, France, Switzerland, and elsewhere. Many of these branches and agencies specialize in dealing in the home currency of their parent bank. A substantial share of the foreign exchange activity of the dealers in the United States is done by these U.S. branches and subsidiaries of foreign banks.

Some, but not all, of the 93 reporting dealers in the United States act as market makers for one or a number of currencies. A market maker is a dealer who regularly quotes both bids and offers for one or more particular currencies and stands ready to make a two-sided market for its customers. Thus, during normal hours a market maker will, in principle, be willing to commit the firm's capital, within limits, to complete both buying and selling transactions at the prices he quotes, and to seek to make a profit on the spread, or difference, between the two prices. In order to make a profit from this activity, the market maker must manage the firm's own inventory and position very carefully, and accurately perceive the short-term trends and prospects of the market. A market maker is more or less continuously in the market, trading with customers and balancing the flow of these activities with offsetting trades on the firm's own account. In foreign exchange, as in other markets, market makers are regarded as helpful to the functioning of the market—contributing to liquidity and short-run price stability, providing useful price information, smoothing imbalances in the flow of business, maintaining the continuity of trading, and making it easier to trade promptly.

2. Financial And Nonfinancial Customers

According to the 1998 survey, as shown in *Figure 4-1*, 49 percent of the foreign exchange trading activity in the over-the-counter market represented "interdealer" transactions, that is, trading by the 93 reporting dealers among themselves and with comparable dealers abroad. Of the remaining 51 percent of total foreign exchange transactions, financial (non-dealer) customers accounted for 31 percent, and non-financial customers 20 percent.

The range of financial and nonfinancial customers includes such counterparties as: smaller commercial banks and investment banks that do not act as major dealers, firms and corporations that are buying or selling foreign exchange because they (or the customers for whom they are acting) are in the process of buying or selling something else (a product, a service, or a financial asset), managers of money funds, mutual funds, hedge

F I G U R E   4 - 1

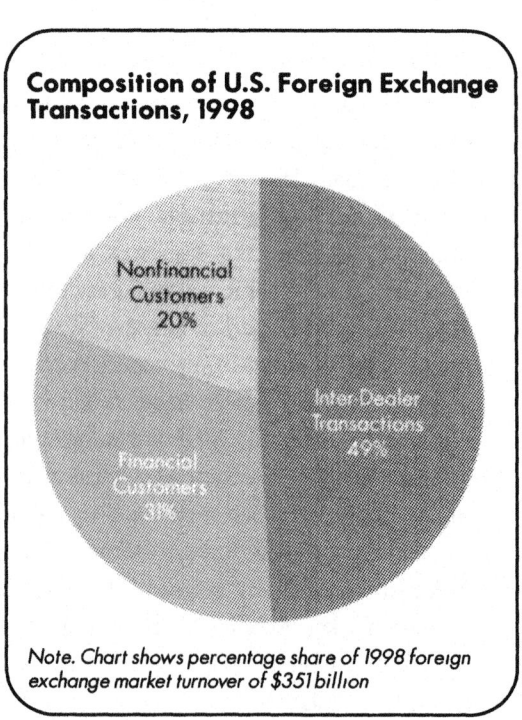

Composition of U.S. Foreign Exchange Transactions, 1998

Nonfinancial Customers 20%

Inter-Dealer Transactions 49%

Financial Customers 31%

Note. Chart shows percentage share of 1998 foreign exchange market turnover of $351 billion

funds, and pension funds; and even high net worth individuals. For such intermediaries and end-users, the foreign exchange transaction is part of the payments process—that is, a means of completing some commercial, investment, speculative, or hedging activity.

Over the years, the universe of foreign exchange end-users has changed markedly, reflecting the changing financial environment. By far the most striking change has been the spectacular growth in the activity of those engaged in international capital movements for investment purposes. A generation ago, with relatively modest overseas investment flows, foreign exchange activity in the United States was focused on international trade in goods and services. Importers and exporters accounted for the bulk of the foreign exchange that was bought from and sold to final customers in the United States as they financed the nation's overseas trade.

But investment to and from overseas—as indicated by the capital flows, cross-border bank claims, and securities transactions reported in Chapter 1—has expanded far more rapidly than has trade. Institutional investors, insurance companies, pension funds, mutual funds, hedge funds, and other investment funds have, in recent years, become major participants in the foreign exchange markets. Many of these investors have begun to take a more global approach to portfolio management. Even though these institutions in the aggregate still hold only a relatively small proportion (5 to 10

percent) of their investments in foreign currency denominated assets, the amounts these institutions control are so large that they have become key players in the foreign exchange market. In the United States, for example, mutual funds have grown to more than $5 trillion in total assets, pension funds are close to $3 trillion, and insurance companies about $2 1/2 trillion. The hedge funds, though far smaller in total assets, also are able to play an important role, given their frequent use of high leverage and, in many cases, their investors' financial strength and higher tolerance for risk.

Given the large magnitudes of these institutions' assets, even a modest shift in emphasis toward foreign investment can mean large increases in foreign exchange transactions. In addition, there has been a tendency among many funds managers worldwide to manage their investments much more actively, and with greater focus on short-term results. Rapid growth in derivatives and the development of new financial instruments also have fostered international investment.

Reflecting these developments, portfolio investment has come to play a very prominent role in the foreign exchange market and accounts for a large share of foreign exchange market activity. The role of portfolio investment may continue to grow rapidly, as fund managers and investors increase the level of funds invested abroad, which is still quite modest, especially relative to the corresponding levels in many other advanced economies.

3. Central Banks

All central banks participate in their nations' foreign exchange markets to some degree, and their operations can be of great importance to those markets. But central banks differ, not only in the extent of their participation, but also in the manner and purposes of their involvement. The role of the Federal Reserve in the foreign exchange market is discussed more fully in Chapter 9.

Intervention operations designed to influence foreign exchange market conditions or the exchange rate represent a critically important aspect of central banks' foreign exchange transactions. However, the intervention practices of individual central banks differ greatly with respect to objectives, approaches, amounts, and tactics.

Unlike the days of the Bretton Woods par value system (before 1971), nations are now free, within broad rules of the IMF, to choose the exchange rate regime they feel best suits their needs. The United States and many other developed and developing nations have chosen an "independently floating" regime, providing for a considerable degree of flexibility in their exchange rates. But a large number of countries continue to peg their currencies, either to the U.S. dollar or some other currency, or to a currency basket or a currency composite, or have chosen some other regime to limit or manage flexibility of the home currency (Figure 4-2). The choice of exchange rate regime determines the basic framework within which each central bank carries out its intervention activities.

The techniques employed by a central bank to maintain an exchange rate that is pegged or closely tied to another currency are straightforward and have limited room for maneuver or change. But for the United States and others with more flexible regimes, the approach to intervention can be

FIGURE 4-2

CLASSIFICATION OF EXCHANGE RATE ARRANGEMENTS, SEPTEMBER 1997*

Regime	Number of Countries
Independently Floating	51
Managed Floating	47
Limited Flexibility	16
European Monetary System[1]	12
Other	4
Pegged to	67
U.S. dollar	21
French franc	15
Other currency	9
Composite[2]	22
Total	181

*The International Monetary Fund classification of exchange rate regimes with "independently floating" representing the highest degree of flexibility, followed by "managed floating"; of the seven largest industrial democracies, four (United States, Japan, Canada, and United Kingdom) belong to the independently floating group, and three (France, Germany, and Italy) participate in the European Monetary System arrangement.

[1]Refers to the arrangement under the European Monetary System covering Austria, Belgium, Denmark, Finland, France, Germany, Ireland, Italy, Luxembourg, Netherlands, Portugal and Spain.

[2]Refers to countries where exchange rates are pegged to various "baskets" of currencies, including two countries (Libya and Myanmar) that peg their currencies to the SDR basket.

varied in many ways—whether and when to intervene, in which currencies and geographic markets, in what amounts, aggressively or less so, openly or discreetly, and in concert with other central banks or not. The resolution of these and other issues depends on an assessment of market conditions and the objectives of the intervention. As discussed in Chapter 9, the United States, operating under the same broad policy guideline over a number of years, has experienced both periods of relatively heavy intervention and periods of minimal activity.

Foreign exchange market intervention is not the only reason central banks buy and sell foreign currencies. Many central banks serve as their government's principal international banker, and handle most, and in some cases all, foreign exchange transactions for the government as well as for other public sector enterprises, such as the post office, electric power utilities, and nationalized airline or railroad. Consequently, even without its own intervention operations, a central bank may be operating in the foreign exchange market in order to acquire or dispose of foreign currencies for some government procurement or investment purpose. A central bank also may seek to accumulate, reallocate among currencies, or reduce its foreign exchange reserve balances. It may be in the market as agent for another central bank, using that other central bank's resources to assist it in influencing that nation's exchange rate. Alternatively, it might be assisting another central bank in acquiring foreign currencies needed for the other central bank's activities or business expenditures.

Thus, for example, the Foreign Exchange Desk of the Federal Reserve Bank of New York engages in intervention operations only occasionally. But it usually is in the market every day, buying and selling foreign currencies, often in modest amounts, for its "customers" (i.e., other central banks, some U.S. agencies, and international institutions). This "customer" business provides a useful service to other central banks or agencies, while also enabling the Desk to stay in close touch with the market for the currencies being traded.

4. Brokers

▶ In the Over-the-Counter Market

The role of a broker in the OTC market is to bring together a buyer and a seller in return for a fee or commission. Whereas a "dealer" acts as principal in a transaction and may take one side of a trade for his firm's account, thus committing the firm's capital, a "broker" is an intermediary who acts as agent for one or both parties in the transaction and, in principle, does not commit capital. The dealer hopes to find the other side to the transaction and earn a spread by closing out the position in a subsequent trade with another party, while the broker relies on the commission received for the service provided (i.e., bringing the buyer and seller together). Brokers do not take positions or face the risk of holding an inventory of currency balances subject to exchange rate fluctuations. In over-the-counter trading, the activity of brokers is confined to the dealers market. Brokers, including "voice" brokers located in the United States and abroad, as well as electronic brokerage systems, handle about one-quarter of all U.S. foreign exchange transactions in the OTC market. The remaining three-quarters takes the form of "direct dealing" between dealers and other institutions in the market. The present

▶ **Voice Brokers**

Skill in carrying out operations for customers and the degree of customers' confidence determine a voice broker's success. To perform their function, brokers must stay in close touch with a large number of dealers and know the rates at which market participants are prepared to buy and sell. With 93 active dealers in New York and a much larger number in London, that can be a formidable task, particularly at times of intense activity and volatile rate movements. Information is the essential ingredient of the foreign exchange market and the player with the latest, most complete, and most reliable information holds the best cards. As one channel, many voice brokers have open telephone lines to many trading desks, so that a bank trader dealing in, say, sterling, can hear over squawk boxes continuous oral reports of the activity of brokers in that currency, the condition of the market, the number of transactions occurring, and the rates at which trading is taking place, though traders do not hear the names of the two banks in the transaction or the specific amounts of the trade.

▶ **Automated Order-Matching, or Electronic Broking Systems**

Until 1992, all brokered business in the U.S. OTC market was handled by voice brokers. But during the past few years, *electronic broker systems* (or automated order-matching systems) have gained a significant share of the market for spot transactions. The two electronic broking systems currently operating in the United States are Electronic Brokerage Systems, or EBS, and Reuters 2000-2. In the 1998 survey, electronic broking accounted for 13 percent of total market volume in the United States, more than double its market share three years earlier. In the brokers market, 57 percent of turnover is now conducted through order-matching systems, compared with 18 percent in 1995.

With these electronic systems, traders can see on their screens the bid and offer rates that are being quoted by potential counterparties acceptable to that trader's institution (as well as quotes available in the market more broadly), match an order, and make the deal electronically, with back offices receiving proper notification.

The electronic broking systems are regarded as fast and reliable. Like a voice broker, they offer a degree of anonymity. The counterparty is not known until the deal is struck, and then only to the other counterparty. Also, the systems can automatically manage credit lines. A trader puts in a credit limit for each counterparty that he is willing to deal with, and when the limit is reached, the system automatically disallows further trades. The fees charged for this computerized service are regarded as competitive. The automated systems are already widely used for certain standardized operations in the spot market, particularly for smaller-sized transactions in the most widely traded currency pairs. Many market observers expect these electronic broking or order-matching systems to expand their activities much further and to develop systems to cover additional products, to the competitive disadvantage, in particular, of the voice brokers. Some observers believe that automated systems and other technological advances have substantially slowed the growth in market turnover by reducing "daisy chaining" and the "recycling" of transactions through the markets, as well as by other means. (Electronic broking is discussed further in Chapter 7.)

▶ **In the Exchange-Traded Market**
In the exchange-traded segment of the market, which covers currency futures and exchange-traded currency options, the institutional structure and the role of brokers are different from those in the OTC market.

In the exchanges, orders from customers are transmitted to a *floor broker*. The floor broker then tries to execute the order on the floor of the exchange (by open outcry), either with another floor broker or with one of the *floor traders*, also called "locals," who are members of the exchange on the trading floor, executing trades for themselves.

Each completed deal is channeled through the clearinghouse of that particular exchange by a clearing member firm. A participant that is not a clearing member firm must have its trades cleared by a clearing member.

The clearinghouse guarantees the performance of both parties, assuring that the long side of every short position will be met, and that the short side of every long position will be met. This requires (unlike in the OTC market) payment of initial and maintenance margins to the clearinghouse (by buyers and sellers of futures and by writers, but not holders, of options). In addition, there is daily marking to market and settlement. Thus, frequent payments to (and receipts from) brokers and clearing members may be called for by customers to meet these daily settlements.

CHAPTER 5

Chapter 3 noted that the United States has both an *over-the-counter* market in foreign

exchange and an *exchange-traded* segment of the market The *OTC* market is the U S

portion of an international OTC network of major dealers—mainly but not exclusively

banks—operating in financial centers around the world, trading with each other and

with customers, via computers, telephones, and other means. The *exchange-traded*

market covers trade in a limited number of foreign exchange products on the floors of

organized exchanges located in Chicago, Philadelphia, and New York.

This chapter describes the foreign exchange products traded in the OTC market. It covers the three "traditional" foreign exchange instruments —*spot*, *outright forwards*, and *FX swaps*, which were the *only* instruments traded before the 1970s, and which still constitute the overwhelming share of all foreign exchange market activity. It also covers two more recent products in which OTC trading has developed since the 1970s—*currency swaps* and *OTC currency options*.

The next chapter describes *currency futures* and *exchange-traded currency options*, which currently are traded in U.S. exchanges.

1. Spot

A *spot* transaction is a straightforward (or "outright") exchange of one currency for another. The spot rate is the current market price, the benchmark price.

Spot transactions do not require *immediate* settlement, or payment "on the spot." By convention, the settlement date, or "value date," is the *second* business day after the "deal date" (or "trade date") on which the transaction is agreed to by the two traders. The two-day period provides ample time for the two parties to confirm the agreement and arrange the clearing and necessary debiting and crediting of bank accounts in various international locations.

Exceptionally, spot transactions between the Canadian dollar and U.S. dollar conventionally are settled *one* business day after the deal, rather than *two* business days later, since Canada is in the same time zone as the United States and an earlier value date is feasible.

It is possible to trade for value dates *in advance* of the spot value date two days hence ("pre-spot" or "ante-spot"). Traders can trade for "value tomorrow," with settlement one business day after the deal date (one day before spot); or even for "cash," with settlement on the deal date (two days before spot). Such transactions are a very small part of the market, particularly same day "cash" transactions for the U.S. dollar against European or Asian currencies, given the time zone differences. Exchange rates for cash or value tomorrow transactions are based on spot rates, but differ from spot, reflecting in part, the fact that interest rate differences between the two currencies affect the cost of earlier payment. Also, pre-spot trades are much less numerous and the market is less liquid.

A spot transaction represents a *direct exchange* of one currency for another, and when executed, leads to transfers through the payment systems of the two countries whose currencies are involved. In a typical spot transaction, Bank A in New York will agree on June 1 to sell $10 million for Deutsche marks to Bank B in Frankfurt at the rate of, say, DEM 1.7320 per dollar, for value June 3. On June 3, Bank B will pay DEM 17.320 million for credit to Bank A's account at a bank in Germany, and Bank A will pay $10 million for credit to Bank B's account at a bank in the United States. The execution of the two payments completes the transaction.

▶ **There is a Buying Price and a Selling Price**
In the foreign exchange market there are always *two prices* for every currency—one price at which sellers of that currency want to sell, and another price at which buyers want to buy. A *market maker* is expected to quote simultaneously for his customers *both* a price at which he is willing to sell and a price at which he is willing to buy standard amounts of any currency for which he is making a market.

▶ **How Spot Rates are Quoted: Direct and Indirect Quotes, European and American Terms**
Exchange rate quotes, as the price of one currency in terms of another, come in two forms: a "direct" quotation is the amount of domestic currency (dollars and cents if you are in the United States) per unit of foreign currency and an "indirect" quotation is the amount of foreign currency per

unit of domestic currency (per dollar if you are in the United States).

The phrase "*American terms*" means a direct quote from the point of view of someone located in the United States. For the dollar, that means that the rate is quoted in *variable amounts of U.S. dollars and cents per one unit of foreign currency (e.g., $0.5774 per DEM1)*. The phrase "*European terms*" means a direct quote from the point of view of someone located in Europe. For the dollar, that means *variable amounts of foreign currency per one U.S. dollar (or DEM 1.7320 per $1)*.

In daily life, most prices are quoted "directly," so when you go to the store you pay x dollars and y cents for one loaf (unit) of bread. For many years, all dollar exchange rates also were quoted directly. That meant dollar exchange rates were quoted in European terms in Europe, and in American terms in the United States. However, in 1978, as the foreign exchange market was integrating into a single global market, for convenience, the practice in the U.S. market was changed—at the initiative of the brokers community—to conform to the European convention. Thus, OTC markets in all countries now quote dollars in European terms against nearly all other currencies (amounts of foreign currency per $1). That means that the dollar is nearly always the *base* currency, one unit of which (one dollar) is being bought or sold for a variable amount of a foreign currency.

There are still exceptions to this general rule, however. In particular, in all OTC markets around the world, the pound sterling continues to be quoted as the base currency against the dollar and other currencies. Thus, market makers and brokers everywhere quote the pound sterling at x dollars and cents per pound, or y DEM per pound, and so forth. The

United Kingdom did not adopt a decimal currency system until 1971, and it was much easier mathematically to quote and trade in terms of variable amounts of foreign currency per pound than the other way around.

Certain currencies historically linked to the British pound—the Irish, Australian, and New Zealand currencies—are quoted in the OTC market in the same way as the pound: variable amounts of dollars and cents per unit. The SDR and the ECU, composite currency units of the IMF and the European Monetary Union, also are quoted in dollars and cents per SDR or ECU. Similarly, it is expected that the euro will be quoted in dollars and cents per euro, at least among dealers. But all other currencies traded in the OTC market are quoted in variable amounts of foreign currency per one dollar.

Direct and indirect quotes are reciprocals, and either can easily be determined from the other. In the United States, the financial press typically reports the quotes both ways, as shown in the excerpt from The New York Times in Figure 5-2 at the end of the chapter.

The third and fourth columns show the quotes for the previous two days in "European terms"— the foreign currency price of one dollar—which is the convention used for most exchange rates by dealers in the OTC market.

The first and second columns show the (reciprocal) quotes for the same two days in American terms—the price in dollars and cents of one unit of each of various foreign currencies— which is the approach sometimes used by traders in dealings with commercial customers, and is also the convention used for quoting dollar exchange rates in the exchange-traded segment of the U.S. foreign exchange market.

▶ **There Is a Base Currency and a Terms Currency**
Every foreign exchange transaction involves two currencies—and it is important to keep straight which is the *base* currency (or *quoted, underlying,* or *fixed* currency) and which is the *terms* currency (or *counter* currency). A trader always buys or sells a fixed amount of the "base" currency—as noted above, most often the dollar—and adjusts the amount of the "terms" currency as the exchange rate changes.

The terms currency is thus the *numerator* and the base currency is the *denominator*. When the numerator increases, the base currency is strengthening and becoming more expensive; when the numerator decreases, the base currency is weakening and becoming cheaper.

In oral communications, the base currency is always stated *first*. For example, a quotation for "dollar-yen" means the dollar is the base and the denominator, and the yen is the terms currency and the numerator; "dollar-swissie" means that the Swiss franc is the terms currency; and "sterling-dollar" (usually called "cable") means that the dollar is the terms currency. Currency codes are also used to denote currency pairs, with the base currency usually presented first, followed by an oblique. Thus "dollar-yen" is *USD/JPY*; "dollar-Swissie" is *USD/CHF*; and "sterling-dollar" is *GBP/USD*.

▶ **Bids and Offers Are for the Base Currency**
Traders *always* think in terms of how much it costs to *buy* or *sell* the *base* currency. A market maker's quotes are *always* presented *from the market maker's point of view*, so the *bid* price is the amount of terms currency that the market maker will pay for a unit of the base currency; the *offer* price is the amount of terms currency the market maker will charge for a unit of the base currency. A market maker asked for a quote on "dollar-swissie" might respond "1.4975-85," indicating a bid price of CHF

1.4975 per dollar and an offer price of CHF 1.4985 per dollar. Usually the market maker will simply give the quote as "75-85," and assume that the counterparty knows that the "big figure" is 1.49. The bid price always is offered *first* (the number on the left), and is *lower* (a smaller amount of terms currency) than the *offer* price (the larger number on the right). This differential is the dealer's *spread*.

▶ Quotes Are in Basis Points

For most currencies, bid and offer quotes are presented to the *fourth* decimal place—that is, to one-hundredth of one percent, or 1/10,000th of the *terms* currency unit, usually called a "pip." However, for a few currency units that are relatively small in absolute value, such as the Japanese yen and the Italian lira, quotes may be carried to *two* decimal places and a "pip" is 1/100 of the terms currency unit. In any market, a "pip" or a "tick" is the smallest amount by which a price can move in that market, and in the foreign exchange market "pip" is the term commonly used.

▶ Cross Rate Trading

Cross rates, as noted in Chapter 3, are exchange rates in which the dollar is neither the base nor the terms currency, such as "mark-yen," in which the DEM is the base currency; and "sterling-mark," in which the pound sterling is the base currency. In cross trades, either currency can be made the base, although there are standard pairs—mark-yen, sterling-swissie, etc. As usual, the base currency is mentioned first.

There are both *derived* cross rates and *directly traded* cross rates. Historically, cross rates were derived from the dollar rates of the two named currencies, even if the transaction was not actually channeled through the dollar. Thus, a cross rate for sterling-yen would be derived from the sterling-dollar and dollar-yen rates. That continues to be the practice for many currency pairs, as described in Box 5.1, but for other pairs, viable markets have developed and direct trading sets the cross rates, within the boundary rates established by the derived cross rate calculations.

BOX 5-1

DERIVING CROSS RATES FROM DOLLAR EXCHANGE RATES

There are simplified, short-cut ways to *derive* cross rates from the dollar exchange rates of the two cross currencies, by cross dividing or by multiplying.

There are *three* cases—the case in which the dollar exchange rates of both of the cross rate currencies are *quoted* "*indirectly*"; the case in which both currencies are *quoted* "*directly*"; and the case in which one is *quoted indirectly and the other is quoted directly.*

▶ **Cass 1.** If *both* of the cross rate currencies are quoted against the dollar in the more common *indirect or European* terms, for example, "dollar-Swiss franc" and "dollar-yen," to get a *Swiss franc-yen* derived cross rate, *cross divide* as follows:

   —for the cross rate *bid*: divide the bid of the cross rate terms currency *by* the offer of the base currency;

   —for the cross rate offer: divide the offer of the terms currency by the bid of the base currency.

Thus, if the dollar-swissie rate is 1.5000-10 and the dollar-yen rate is 100.00-10, for a Swiss franc-yen derived cross rate: the bid would be 100.00 divided by 1.5010, or 66.6223 yen per Swiss franc, and the offer would be 100.10 divided by 1.5000, or 66.7333 yen per Swiss franc.

▶ **Case 2.** If *both* of the two cross rate currencies are quoted against the dollar in the less common *direct, or American terms*, (i.e., reciprocal, or "upside down") for example, "sterling-dollar" and "Irish punt-dollar," to get a *sterling-Irish punt* derived *cross rate, cross divide* as follows:

—for the cross rate *bid*: divide the offer of the cross rate terms currency *into* the bid of the base currency;
—for the cross rate *offer*: divide the bid of the terms currency *into* the offer of the base currency.

Thus, if the sterling-dollar rate is 1.6000-10 and the Irish punt-dollar rate is 1.4000-10, for a *sterling-Irish punt* derived cross rate: the bid would be 1.6000 divided by 1.4010, or 1.1420 Irish punt per pound sterling, and the offer would be 1.6010 divided by 1.4000, or *1.1436* punt per pound sterling.

▶ **Case 3.** If the two cross currencies are quoted in *different terms*, i.e., one in indirect or European terms (for example, "dollar-yen") and one in direct or American terms (for example, "sterling-dollar"), to get a *sterling-yen* derived cross rate, *multiply* as follows:

—for the cross rate *bid*: multiply the bid of the cross rate terms currency by the bid of the base currency;
—for the cross rate *offer*: multiply the offer of the terms currency by the offer of the base currency.

Thus, if the sterling-dollar rate is 1.6000-10 and the dollar-yen rate is 100.00-10, for a *sterling-yen* derived cross rate: the bid would be 1.6000 multiplied by 100.00, or *160.00* yen per pound, and the offer would be 1.6010 multiplied by 100.10, or *160.26* yen per pound.

These derived, or conceptual, prices are the "boundary" prices (beyond these prices, risk-free arbitrage is possible). But they are not necessarily the prices, or the spreads, that will prevail in the market, and traders may have to shave their spreads to compete with cross rates being quoted and perhaps directly traded. For example, there are likely to be some players who have one or another of the "component" currencies in balances they are willing to use, or a trader may want to use the transaction to accumulate balances of a particular currency.

The same general rules are used to derive cross rates through a vehicle currency other than the U.S. dollar. Thus, if two cross currencies are quoted against the vehicle in the same terms, divide as appropriate by or into the base of the pair; if in *different* terms, multiply.

During the 1980s and '90s, there was a very large expansion of *direct* cross trading, in which the dollar was not involved either as metric or as medium of exchange. Much of this direct cross trading activity involved the Deutsche mark. Direct trading activity between the mark and other European currencies developed to the point where most trading of currencies in the European Monetary System took place directly through cross rates, and the most widely direct-traded crosses came to be used to quote rates for other, less widely traded currency pairs. By the mid-1990s, mark-yen, sterling-mark, mark-French franc (or mark-Paris), and mark-Swiss all were very actively traded pairs.

Deutsche mark cross trading with European currencies developed to the point where rates in the New York market for dollar-lira, dollar-French franc, etc., were usually calculated from the mark-lira, mark-French franc, etc., particularly during the afternoon in New York, when European markets were closed.

As direct cross currency trading between non-dollar currencies expanded, new trading opportunities developed. Various arbitrage opportunities became possible between the cross rate markets and the direct dollar markets. Traders had more choices than they had in a system in which the dollar was virtually always the vehicle currency.

With the launching of the euro in 1999, major structural changes in cross trading activity can be expected. With the euro replacing a number of European currencies, much of the earlier cross trading will no longer be required. What role the euro itself may play as a vehicle currency remains to be seen.

2. Outright Forwards

An *outright forward* transaction, like a spot transaction, is a straightforward single purchase/sale of one currency for another. The only difference is that spot is settled, or delivered, on a value date no later than two business days after the deal date, while *outright forward* is settled on any pre-agreed date three or more business days after the deal date. Dealers use the term "outright forward" to make clear that it is a single purchase or sale on a future date, and not part of an "FX swap" (described later).

There is a specific exchange rate for each forward maturity of a currency, almost always different from the spot rate. The exchange rate at which the outright forward transaction is executed is fixed at the outset. No money necessarily changes hands until the transaction actually takes place, although dealers may require some customers to provide collateral in advance.

Outright forwards can be used for a variety of purposes—covering a known future expenditure, hedging, speculating, or any number of commercial, financial, or investment purposes. The instrument is very flexible, and forward transactions can be tailored and customized to meet the particular needs of a customer with respect to currency, amount, and maturity date. Of course, customized forward contracts for non-standard dates or amounts are generally more

costly and less liquid, and more difficult to reverse or modify in the event of need than are standard forward contracts. Also, forward contracts for minor currencies and exotic currencies can be more difficult to arrange and more costly.

Outright forwards in major currencies are available over-the-counter from dealers for standard contract periods or "straight dates" (one, two, three, six, and twelve months); dealers tend to deal with each other on straight dates. However, customers can obtain "odd-date" or "broken-date" contracts for deals falling between standard dates, and traders will determine the rates through a process of interpolation. The agreed-upon maturity can range from a few days to months or even two or three years ahead, although very long-dated forwards are rare because they tend to have a large bid-asked spread and are relatively expensive.

▶ **Relationship of Forward to Spot—Covered Interest Rate Parity**
The *forward* rate for any two currencies is a function of their spot rate and the *interest rate differential* between them. For major currencies, the interest rate differential is determined in the Eurocurrency deposit market. Under the *covered interest rate parity principle*, and with the opportunity of arbitrage, the forward rate will

ALL ABOUT...

tend toward an equilibrium point at which any difference in Eurocurrency interest rates between the two currencies would be exactly offset, or neutralized, by a premium or discount in the forward rate.

If, for example, six-month Euro-dollar deposits pay interest of 5 percent per annum, and six-month Euro-yen deposits pay interest of 3 percent per annum, *and* if there is no premium or discount on the forward yen against the forward dollar, there would be an opportunity for "round-tripping" and an arbitrage profit with no exchange risk. Thus, it would pay to borrow yen at 3 percent, sell the yen spot for dollars and simultaneously resell dollars forward for yen six months hence, meanwhile investing the dollars at the higher interest rate of 5 percent for the six-month period. This arbitrage opportunity would tend to drive up the forward exchange rate of the yen relative to the dollar (or force some other adjustment) until there were an equal return on the two investments after taking into account the cost of covering the forward exchange risk.

Similarly, if short-term dollar investments and short-term yen investments both paid the same interest rate, and if there were a premium on the forward yen against the forward dollar, there would once again be an opportunity for an arbitrage profit with no exchange risk, which again would tend to reduce the premium on the forward yen (or force some other adjustment) until there were an equal return on the two investments after covering the cost of the forward exchange risk.

In this state of equilibrium, or condition of covered interest rate parity, an investor (or a borrower) who operates in the forward exchange market will realize the same domestic return (or pay the same domestic cost) whether investing (borrowing) in his domestic currency or in a foreign currency, net of the costs of forward exchange rate cover. The forward exchange rate should offset, or neutralize, the interest rate differential between the two currencies.

The forward rate in the *market* can deviate from this theoretical, or implied, equilibrium rate derived from the interest rate differential to the extent that there are significant costs, restrictions, or market inefficiencies that prevent arbitrage from taking place in a timely manner. Such constraints could take the form of transaction costs, information gaps, government regulations, taxes, unavailability of comparable investments (in terms of risk, maturity, amount, etc.), and other impediments or imperfections in the capital markets. However, today's large and deregulated foreign exchange markets and Eurocurrency deposit markets for the dollar and other heavily traded currencies are generally free of major impediments.

❯ Role of the Offshore Deposit Markets for Euro-Dollars and Other Currencies

Forward contracts have existed in commodity markets for hundreds of years. In the foreign exchange markets, forward contracts have been traded since the nineteenth century, and the concept of interest arbitrage has been understood and described in economic literature for a long time. (Keynes wrote about it and practiced it in the 1920s.) But it was the development of the offshore *Eurocurrency deposit markets*—the markets for offshore deposits in dollars and other major currencies—in the 1950s and '60s that facilitated and refined the process of interest rate arbitrage in practice and brought it to its present high degree of efficiency, closely linking the foreign exchange market and the money markets of the major nations, and equalizing returns through the two channels.

With large and liquid offshore deposit markets in operation, and with information transfers greatly improved and accelerated, it became much easier and quicker to detect any significant deviations from covered interest rate parity, and to take advantage of any such arbitrage opportunities. From the outset, deposits in these offshore markets were generally free of taxes, reserve requirements, and other government restrictions. The offshore deposit markets in London and elsewhere quickly became very convenient for, and closely attached to, the foreign exchange market. These offshore Eurocurrency markets for the dollar and other major currencies were, from the outset, handled by the banks' foreign exchange trading desks, and many of the same business practices were adopted. These deposits trade over the telephone like foreign exchange, with a bid/offer spread, and they have similar settlement dates and other trading conventions. Many of the same counterparties participate in both markets, and credit risks are similar. It is thus no surprise that the interest rates in the offshore deposit market in London came to be used for interest parity and arbitrage calculations and operations. Dealers keep a very close eye on the interest rates in the London market when quoting forward rates for the major currencies in the foreign exchange market. For currencies not traded in the offshore Eurocurrency deposit markets in London and elsewhere, deposits in domestic money markets may provide a channel for arbitraging the forward exchange rate and interest rate differentials.

▶ How Forward Rates are Quoted by Traders

Although spot rates are quoted in *absolute* terms—say, x yen per dollar—forward rates, as a matter of convenience are quoted among dealers in *differentials*—that is, in premiums or discounts from the spot rate. The premium or discount is measured in "points," which represent the interest rate differential between the two currencies for the period of the forward, converted into foreign exchange. Specifically, points are the amount of foreign exchange (or basis points) that will neutralize the interest rate differential between two currencies for the applicable period. Thus, if interest rates are *higher* for currency A than currency B, the points will be the number of basis points to *subtract* from currency A's spot exchange rate to yield a forward exchange rate that neutralizes or offsets the interest rate differential (see Box 5-2). Most forward contracts are arranged so that, at the outset, the present value of the contract is zero.

Traders in the market thus know that for *any* currency pair, if the base currency earns a

---

BOX 5-2

CALCULATING FORWARD PREMIUM/DISCOUNT POINTS

▶ Formulas for calculating forward premiums and discounts, expressed as points of the spot rate, equate the two cash flows so that the forward premium or discount neutralizes the differential between interest rates in the two currencies. A generalized formula is:

$$\text{Points} = \text{Spot Rate} \left[\frac{1 + \text{Terms Currency Interest Rate} \times \frac{\text{Forward Days}}{\text{Interest Rate Year}}}{1 + \text{Base Currency Interest Rate} \times \frac{\text{Forward Days}}{\text{Interest Rate Year}}} - 1 \right]$$

▶ Thus, if the dollar is the base currency, with a Euro-dollar (offshore) interest rate of 5 percent, and the Swiss franc is the terms currency, with 6 percent interest in the offshore market, and the spot rate is CHF 1.6000 per dollar, then the points for a six-month (181-day) forward rate would be 78. (Most currencies use a 360-day interest rate year, except the pound sterling and a few others, which use a 365-day year.)

$$\text{Points} = 1.6000 \frac{1 + \left[.06 \times \frac{(181)}{(360)} \right]}{1 + \left[.05 \times \frac{(180)}{(360)} \right]} - 1 = 78$$

The six month outright forward rate would be CHF 1.6078 per dollar.

▶ The above generalized formula takes no account of the differences between borrowing and lending rates in the offshore deposit market. In pricing possible forward transactions, a trader would take account of those differences, calculate the costs of putting together the deal, determine the "boundary" rates, and perhaps shade the price to reflect competitive quotes, perspectives on market performance, the trader's own portfolio of existing contracts, and other factors.

higher interest rate than the terms currency, the base currency will trade at a forward *discount*, or below the spot rate; and if the base currency earns a *lower* interest rate than the terms currency, the base currency will trade at a forward *premium*, or above the spot rate. Whichever side of the transaction the trader is on, the trader won't gain (or lose) from *both* the interest rate differential and the forward premium/discount. A trader who *loses* on the interest rate will *earn* the forward premium, and vice versa.

Traders have long used rules of thumb and shortcuts for calculating whether to add or subtract the points. Points are subtracted from the spot rate when the interest rate of the base currency is the *higher* one, since the base currency should trade at a forward *discount*; points are added when the interest rate of the base currency is the lower one, since the base currency should trade at a forward *premium*. Another rule of thumb is that the points must be *added* when the small number comes first in the quote of the differential,

but *subtracted* when the larger number comes first. For example, the spot CHF might be quoted at "1.5020- 30," and the 3-month forward at "40-60" (to be added) or "60-40" (to be subtracted). Also, the spread will always *grow larger* when shifting from the spot quote to the forward quote. Screens now show positive and negative signs in front of points, making the process easier still.

▶ **Non-Deliverable Forwards (NDFs)**

In recent years, markets have developed for some currencies in "non-deliverable forwards." This instrument is in concept similar to an outright forward, except that there is no physical delivery or transfer of the local currency. Rather, the agreement calls for settlement of the net amount in dollars or other major transaction currency. NDFs can thus be arranged offshore without the need for access to the local currency markets, and they broaden hedging opportunities against exchange rate risk in some currencies otherwise considered unhedgeable. Use of NDFs with respect to certain currencies in Asia and elsewhere is growing rapidly.

3. FX Swaps

In the spot and outright forward markets, one currency is traded outright for another, but in the FX swap market, one currency is swapped for another for a period of time, and then swapped back, creating an exchange and re-exchange.

An *FX swap* has two separate legs settling on two different value dates, even though it is arranged as a single transaction and is recorded in the turnover statistics as a single transaction. The two counterparties agree to exchange two currencies at a particular rate on one date (the "near date") and to reverse payments, almost always at a different rate, on a specified subsequent date (the "far date"). Effectively, it is a spot transaction and an outright forward transaction going in opposite directions, or else two outright forwards with different settlement dates, and going in opposite directions. If both dates are less than one month from the deal date, it is a "short-dated swap"; if one or both dates are one month or more from the deal date, it is a "forward swap."

The two legs of an FX swap can, in principle, be attached to any pair of value dates. In practice, a limited number of standard maturities account for most transactions. The first leg usually occurs on the spot value date, and for about two-thirds of all FX swaps the second leg occurs within a week. However, there are FX swaps with longer maturities. Among dealers, most of these are arranged for even or straight dates—e.g., one week, one month, three months—but odd or broken dates are also traded for customers.

The FX swap is a standard instrument that has long been traded in the over-the-counter market. Note that it provides for one exchange and one re-exchange only, and is not a stream of payments. The FX swap thus differs from the *interest rate swap*, which provides for an exchange of a stream of interest payments in the same currency but with no exchange of principal; it also differs from the *currency swap* (described later), in which counterparties exchange and re-exchange principal and streams of fixed or floating interest payments in two different currencies.

In the *spot and outright forward markets*, a fixed amount of the base currency (most often the dollar) is always traded for a variable amount of the terms currency (most often a non-dollar currency). However, in the *FX swap market*, a trade for a fixed amount of *either* currency can be arranged.

There are *two* kinds of FX swaps: a *buy/sell* swap, which means buying the fixed, or base, currency on the near date and selling it on the far date; and a *sell/buy* swap, which means selling the fixed currency on the near date and buying it on the far date. If, for example, a trader bought a fixed amount of pounds sterling spot for dollars (the exchange) and sold those pounds sterling six months forward for dollars (the re-exchange), that would be called a *buy/sell sterling swap*.

▶ Why FX Swaps Are Used

The popularity of FX swaps reflects the fact that banks and others in the dealer, or interbank, market often find it useful to shift temporarily into or out of one currency in exchange for a second currency without incurring the exchange rate risk of holding an open position or exposure in the currency that is temporarily held. This avoids a change in currency exposure, and differs from the spot or outright forward, where the purpose is to change a currency exposure. The use of FX swaps is similar to actual borrowing and lending of currencies on a collateralized basis. FX swaps provide a way of using the foreign exchange markets as a funding instrument and an alternative to borrowing and lending in the Euro-dollar and other offshore markets. They are widely used by traders and other market participants for managing liquidity and shifting delivery dates, for hedging, speculation, taking positions on interest rates, and other purposes.

❱ Pricing FX Swaps

The cost of an FX swap is determined by the interest rate differential between the two swapped currencies. Just as in the case of outright forwards, arbitrage and the principle of covered interest rate parity will operate to make the cost of an FX swap equal to the foreign exchange value of the interest rate differential between the two currencies for the period of the swap.

The cost of an FX swap is measured by swap points, or the foreign exchange equivalent of the interest rate differential between two currencies for the period. The difference between the amounts of interest that can be earned on the two currencies during the period of the swap can be calculated by formula (see Box 5-4). The counterparty who holds for the period of the swap the currency that pays the *higher* interest rate will *pay* the points, neutralizing the interest rate differential and equalizing the return on the two currencies; and the counterparty who holds the currency that pays the *lower* interest will *earn* or receive the

points. At the outset, the present value of the FX swap contract is usually arranged to be zero.

The same conditions prevail with an FX swap as with an outright forward—a trader who pays the points in the forward also pays them in the FX swap; a trader who earns the points in the forward also earns them in the FX swap.

For most currencies, swap points are carried to the fourth decimal place. A dollar-swissie swap quoted at 244-221 means that the dealer will buy the dollar forward at his spot bid rate less 0.0244 (in Swiss francs), and sell the dollar forward at his spot offer rate less 0.0221 (in Swiss francs), yielding an (additional) spread of 23 points (or 0.0023).

The FX swap is the difference between the spot and the outright forward (or the difference between the two outright forwards). When you trade an FX swap you are trading the interest rate differential between the two currencies. The FX swap is a very flexible and convenient instrument that is used for a variety of funding, hedging, position management, speculation, and other purposes. FX swaps are extremely popular among OTC interbank dealers, and now account for nearly half of total turnover in the U.S. OTC foreign exchange market. Among its uses are those described in Box 5-3:

─────────── **BOX 5-3**

SOME USES OF FX SWAPS

Managing positions and changing settlement dates. FX swaps can be very helpful in managing day-to-day positions. Of particular convenience and interest to professional market making and dealing institutions are the "spot-next" swap and the "tom-next" swap, which are used by traders to roll over settlements and to balance maturing buys and sells of particular currencies in their books. A dealer who knows on, say June 1, that he has to pay out a certain

(continued on page 42)

BOX 5-3

(continued from page 41)

currency on June 3, may find it convenient or profitable to extend the settlement for a day, for example, when he may be scheduled to receive balances of that currency. The dealer can enter into a "spot-next" swap on the deal date, June 1, and extend the June 3 settlement to June 4. Alternatively, on June 2, the day before the June 3 settlement, the dealer might arrange a "tom-next" swap, to extend that settlement until June 4,[3] which is the spot settlement date for June 2, and a more liquid market. The cost of these one-day swaps would reflect the points (the value of one day's interest differential), or "cost of carry," which would be added to or subtracted from the spot rate. If it then looked as though a June 4 settlement would be difficult, the dealer might roll over the transaction for another day, or longer.

The interest rate differential is also important in calculating "pre-spot" rates—"value tomorrow" transactions, which are settled *one* day *before* spot and "cash," which are settled *two* days *before* spot, or on the deal date.

To calculate (approximate) "pre-spot" rates, you work *backwards*. Thus, assume that dollar-swissie were trading spot at 1.5000-10. Assume that the points for a "tom-next" swap were 3/5, reflecting one day's interest rate differential—the price of extending settlement from day 2 to day 3. To calculate a "value tomorrow" quote—shifting settlement from day 3 to day 2, you would turn the points around (to 5/3) and reverse the sign (in this case subtract them from, rather than add them to, the spot rate), for a quote of *1.4995-97*. (In shifting a settlement *forward*, the higher interest rate currency moves to *discount*; in shifting *backward* to "cash" or "value tomorrow," the higher interest rate currency moves to *premium*.)

Hedging interest rate differential risk. A dealer, for example, who has agreed to buy pounds sterling one year forward faces both an exchange rate risk (that the exchange rate may change) and an interest rate differential risk (that the interest rate differential on which the transaction was priced may change). The dealer can offset the *exchange rate risk* by selling sterling spot (to offset the forward purchase), but he would still have an *interest rate differential risk*. That risk can be offset in two ways: either by borrowing and investing in the off-shore deposit (Euro-currency) markets, or by entering into a new swap (an "unwind") that is the opposite of his outstanding position (that is, the trader can enter into a *buy/sell sterling swap* for a one-year period to offset the position resulting from his forward sterling purchase and spot sterling sale). If neither of the two interest rates nor the spot rate has changed between the time of the trader's initial forward purchase of sterling and the time when the trader's hedging activities are put in place, the trader can cover risk in *either* the FX swap market or the offshore deposit market—the trader has a "perfect" hedge—but the swap may be carried "off-balance-sheet" and thus may be "lighter" on the trader's balance sheet than the borrowing and lending.

Speculating on interest rate differentials. A dealer who expects an interest rate differential to *wide*n would enter into an FX swap in which the dealer *pays* the swap points now (when the differential is small), and—after the interest rate differential has widened—would then enter into another FX swap in the opposite direction (an unwind), in which case the trader would *earn* more swap points from the wider differential than he is paying on the initial swap. A trader who expects interest rate differentials to *narrow* would do the reverse—arrange swaps in which he *earns* the swap points now, when the differential is wide, and *pays* the swap points later, after the differential narrows.

Arbitraging the foreign exchange market and the interest rate market. When the two markets are in equilibrium, a dealer may be more or less indifferent whether he invests through the offshore deposit market (borrowing/lending currencies) or through the foreign exchange market (FX swaps). But there are times when swap points in the foreign exchange market are *not* precisely equivalent to interest rate differentials in the offshore deposit market, and arbitrageurs can use FX swaps together with deposit borrowing and lending operations to fund in the lower-cost market and invest in the higher-return market.

BOX 5-4

CALCULATING FX SWAP POINTS

A market maker will calculate swap points on the basis of borrowing and lending rates in the offshore deposit markets:

$$\text{A. Bid Side Swap Points} = \text{Spot Rate} \left[\frac{1 + \left(\text{ODBRTC} \times \frac{\text{Swap Days}}{360 \text{ or } 365} \right)}{1 + \left(\text{ODLRBC} \times \frac{\text{Swap Days}}{360 \text{ or } 365} \right)} - 1 \right]$$

$$\text{B. Offer Side Swap Points} = \text{Spot Rate} \left[\frac{1 + \left(\text{ODLRTC} \times \frac{\text{Swap Days}}{360 \text{ or } 365} \right)}{1 + \left(\text{ODBRBC} \times \frac{\text{Swap Days}}{360 \text{ or } 365} \right)} - 1 \right]$$

where ODBRTC = offshore deposit borrowing rate in terms currency, ODLRTC = offshore deposit lending rate in base currency, ODBRBC = Euro borrow rate in base currency, and ODLRBC = offshore deposit lending rate in base currency. Assume that offshore deposit $ rates = 5 - 5.25, offshore deposit DEM rates = 6.25 - 6.50, the swap period = 62 days, and the spot rate = DEM 1.600 per dollar. Then, swap points can be calculated as:

$$\text{A. Bid Side Points} = 1.600 \left[\frac{1 + \left(.0625 \times \frac{62}{360} \right)}{1 + \left(.0525 \times \frac{62}{360} \right)} - 1 \right] = \underline{28}$$

$$\text{B. Offer Side Points} = 1.600 \left[\frac{1 + \left(.0650 \times \frac{62}{360} \right)}{1 + \left(.05 \times \frac{62}{360} \right)} - 1 \right] = \underline{41}$$

(continued on page 44)

—————————— **BOX 5-4**

(continued from page 43)

Based on these calculations, the market makers' spread would be 28-41. You *add* when the number on the left is *smaller*; thus

Bid: 1.6000 + .0028 = 1.6028
Offer: 1.6000 + .0041 = 1.6041

4. Currency Swaps

A *currency swap* is structurally different from the FX- *swap* described above. In a typical *currency* swap, counterparties will (a) exchange equal initial principal amounts of two currencies at the spot exchange rate, (b) exchange *a stream of fixed or floating interest rate payments in their swapped currencies* for the agreed period of the swap, and then (c) re-exchange the principal amount at maturity at the initial spot exchange rate. Sometimes, the initial exchange of principal is omitted. Sometimes, instead of exchanging interest payments, a "difference check" is paid by one counterparty to the other to cover the net obligation.

The currency swap provides a mechanism for shifting a loan from one currency to another, or shifting the currency of an asset. It can be used, for example, to enable a company to borrow in a currency different from the currency it needs for its operations, and to receive protection from exchange rate changes with respect to the loan.

The currency swap is closely related to the *interest rate swap*. There are, however, major differences in the two instruments. An interest rate swap is an exchange of interest payment streams of differing character (e.g., fixed rate interest for floating), but in the *same currency*, and involves no exchange of principal. The currency swap is in concept an interest rate swap in more than one currency, and has existed since the 1960s. The interest rate swap became popular in the early 1980s; it subsequently has become an almost indispensable instrument in the financial tool box.

Currency swaps come in various forms. One variant is the *fixed-for-fixed* currency swap, in which the interest rates on the periodic interest payments of the two currencies are fixed at the outset for the life of the swap. Another variant is the *fixed-for-floating* swap, also called *cross-currency swap*, or *currency coupon swap*, in which the interest rate in one currency is floating (e.g., based on LIBOR) and the interest rate in the other is fixed. It is also possible to arrange *floating-for-floating* currency swaps, in which both interest rates are floating.

▶ **Purposes of Currency Swaps**
The motivations for the various forms of currency swap are similar to those that generate a demand for interest rate swaps. The incentive may arise from a comparative advantage that a borrowing company has in a particular currency or capital market. It may result from a company's desire to diversify and spread its borrowing around to

different capital markets, or to shift a cash flow from foreign currencies. It may be that a company cannot gain access to a particular capital market. Or, it may reflect a move to avoid exchange controls, capital controls, or taxes. Any number of possible "market imperfections" or pricing inconsistencies provide opportunities for arbitrage.

Before currency swaps became popular, *parallel loans* and *back-to-back loans* were used by market participants to circumvent exchange controls and other impediments. Offsetting loans in two different currencies might be arranged between two parties; for example, a U.S. firm might make a dollar loan to a French firm in the United States, and the French firm would lend an equal amount to the U.S. firm or its affiliate in France. Such structures have now largely been abandoned in favor of currency swaps.

Because a currency swap, like an interest rate swap, is structurally similar to a forward, it can be seen as an exchange and re-exchange of principal plus a "portfolio of forwards"—a series of forward contracts, one covering each period of interest payment. The currency swap is part of the wave of financial derivative instruments that became popular during the 1980s and '90s. But currency swaps have gained only a modest share of the foreign exchange business. It has been suggested that the higher risk and related capital costs of instruments involving an exchange of principal may in part account for this result.[4] In the 1998 global turnover survey, turnover in currency swaps by reporting dealers was estimated at $10 billion per day. In the United States, turnover was $1.4 billion, well behind the United Kingdom—at $5 billion—and six other countries.

5. Over - The - Counter Foreign Currency Options

A foreign exchange or currency option contract gives the buyer the *right*, but not the *obligation*, to buy (or sell) a specified amount of one currency for another at a specified price on (in some cases, on or before) a specified date. Options are unique in that the right to execute will be exercised only if it is in the holder's interest to do so. That differs from a *forward* contract, in which the parties are obligated to execute the transaction on the maturity date, and it differs from a *futures* contract, in which the parties are obligated, in principle to transact at maturity, but that obligation easily can be—and normally is—bought out and liquidated before the maturity or delivery date.

A *call* option is the right, but not the obligation, to buy the underlying currency, and a

put option is the right, but not the obligation, to sell the underlying currency. All currency option trades involve two sides—the purchase of one currency and the sale of another—so that a *put* to sell pounds sterling for dollars at a certain price is also a *call* to buy dollars for pounds sterling at that price. The purchased currency is the call side of the trade, and the sold currency is the put side of the trade. The party who purchases the option is the holder or buyer, and the party who creates the option is the seller or writer. The price at which the underlying currency may be bought or sold is the exercise, or strike, price. The option premium is the price of the option that the buyer pays to the writer. In exchange for paying the option premium up front, the buyer gains insurance against adverse movements in the underlying spot exchange rate

CHART 5-1

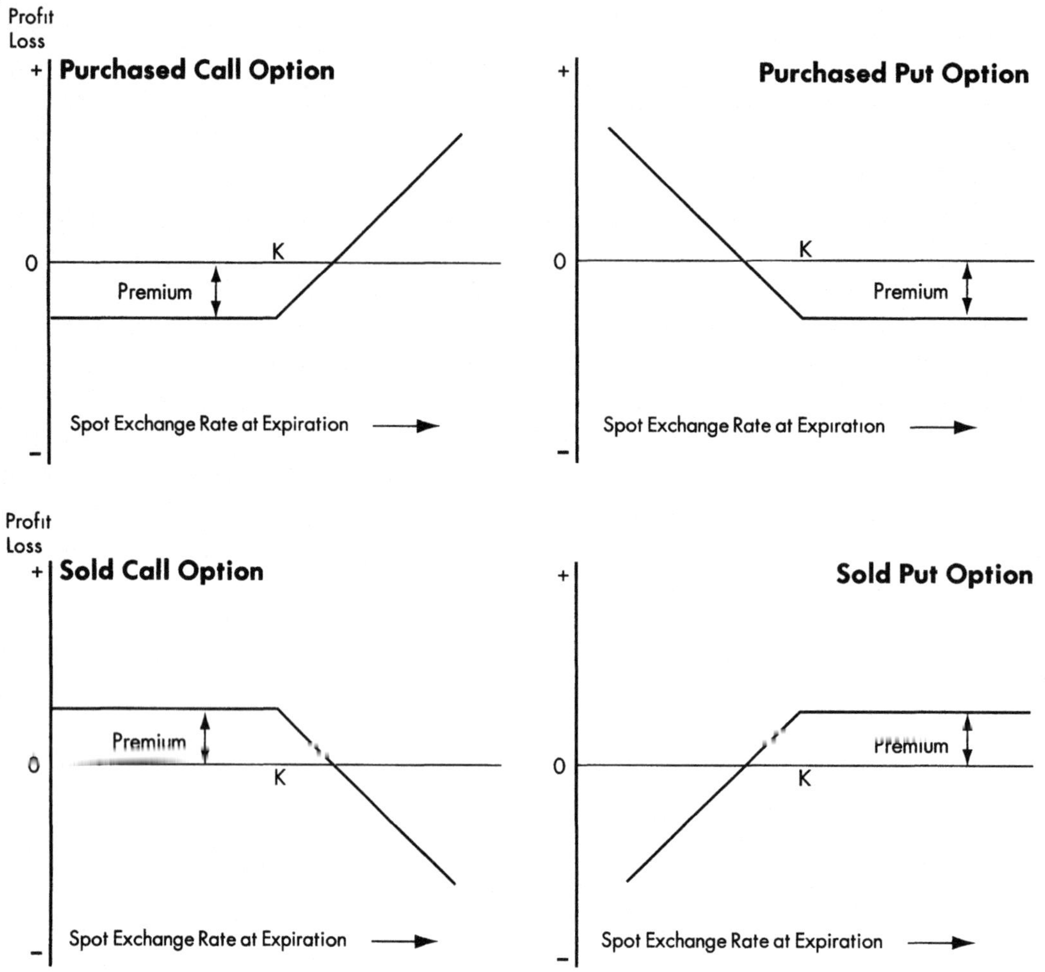

Note: These figures depict the net value of an option contract at expiration as a function of the underlying exchange rate The vertical axis represents the net value of the contract, and the exchange rate (price of the foreign currency) is on the horizontal axis The strike price is at point K

while retaining the opportunity to benefit from favorable movements. The option writer, on the other hand, is exposed to unbounded risk—although the writer can (and typically does) seek to protect himself through hedging or offsetting transactions.

In general, options are written either "European style," which may be exercised only on the expiration date, or "American style," which may be exercised at any time prior to, and including, the expiration date. The American option is at least as valuable as the European option, since it provides the buyer with more opportunities, but is analytically more complex. American calls on the higher interest rate currency are likely to be more valuable than the equivalent European option. The bulk of trading in the OTC interbank market consists of European options, while American options are standard on some of the exchanges.

CHART 5-2

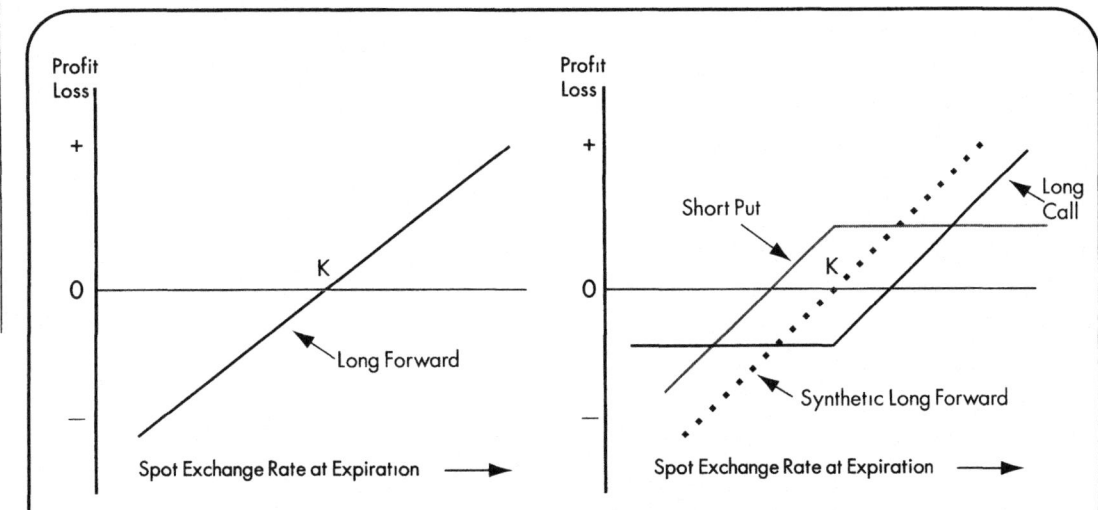

Note. These figures show how the combination of a purchased call option and a sold put option replicates the payoff from a forward contract In the right hand panel, the net payoff from the options equals the dotted line, which is identical to the payoff from a forward contract (depicted in the left hand panel)

The option is one of the most basic financial instruments. All derivatives, including the various derivative financial products developed in recent years—the many forms of forwards, futures, swaps, and options—are based either on *forwards* or on *options*; and *forwards* and *options*, notwithstanding their differences, are related to each other. A *forward* can be created synthetically from a combination of European *options*: Buying a call option and selling a put option (long a call, short a put) on a currency with strike prices at the forward rate provides the same risk position as buying a forward contract on that currency. At expiration, the payoff profiles of the forward and the synthetic forward made up of the two options would be the same: The holder would receive the same payoff whether he held the forward or the combination of two options.

As a financial instrument, the option has a long history. But *foreign exchange* options trading first began to flourish in the 1980s, fostered by an international environment of fluctuating exchange rates, volatile markets, deregulation, and extensive financial innovation. The trading of currency options was initiated in U.S. commodity exchanges and subsequently was introduced into the over-the-counter market. However, options still account for only a small share of total foreign exchange trading.

An over-the-counter foreign exchange option is a bilateral contract between two parties. In contrast to the exchange-traded options market (described later), in the OTC market, no clearinghouse stands between the two parties, and there is no regulatory body establishing trading rules.

Also, in contrast to the exchange-traded options market, which trades in standardized contracts and amounts, for a limited number of currency pairs, and for selected maturity dates, an OTC option can be tailored to meet the special needs of an institutional investor for particular features to satisfy its investment and hedging objectives. But while OTC options contracts can be customized, a very large share of the OTC market consists of generic, or "plain vanilla," options written for major currencies in standard amounts and for even dates.

OTC options are typically written for much larger amounts than exchange-traded options—an average OTC option is $30-$40 million equivalent—and a much broader range of currencies is covered. The volume of OTC options is far greater than that of exchange-traded options; indeed, the OTC market accounts for about four-fifths of the total foreign exchange options traded in the United States.

The two options markets, OTC and exchange-traded, are competitors to some extent, but they also complement each other. Traders use both markets in determining the movement of prices, and are alert to any arbitrage opportunities that may develop between the two markets. Dealers in the OTC market may buy and sell options on the organized exchanges as part of the management of their own OTC positions, hedging or laying off part of an outstanding position in an exchange market.

▶ **The Pricing of Currency Options**
It is relatively easy to determine the value of a European option at its expiration. The value of a European option at expiration is its intrinsic value—the absolute amount by which the strike price of the option is more advantageous to the holder that the spot exchange rate. If at expiration the strike price is *more advantageous* than the spot rate of the underlying, the option is "in the money"; if the difference between the strike price and the spot rate is *zero*, the position is "at the money"; if the strike price is *less advantageous* than the spot rate, the option is "out of the money."

Determining the price of an option *prior* to expiration, on the other hand, is much more

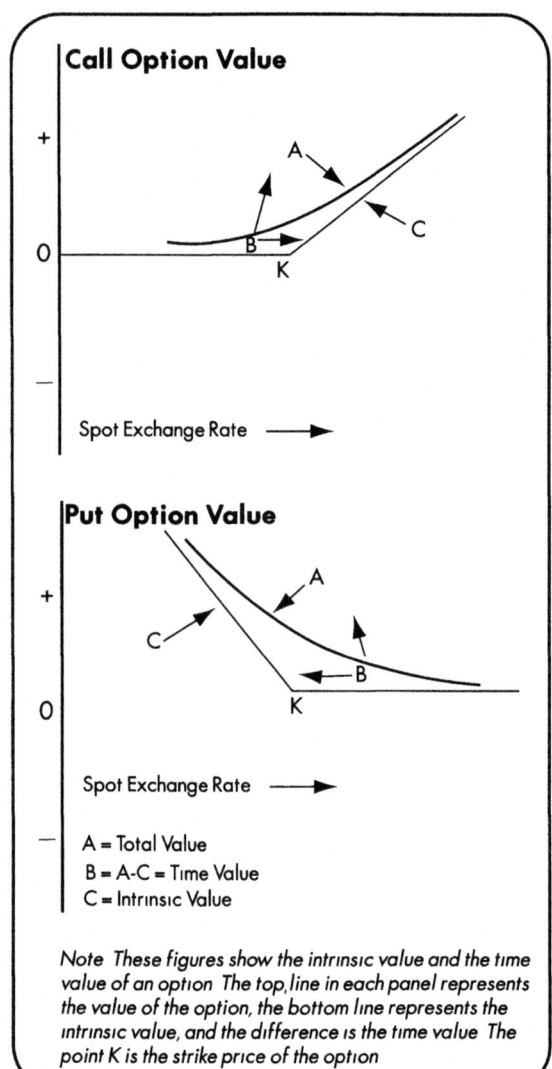

CHART 5-3

Note These figures show the intrinsic value and the time value of an option The top line in each panel represents the value of the option, the bottom line represents the intrinsic value, and the difference is the time value The point K is the strike price of the option

difficult. Before expiration, the total value of an option is based, not only on its *intrinsic* value (reflecting the difference between the strike price and the then current exchange rate), but also on what is called its *time* value, which is the additional value that the market places on the option, reflecting the time remaining to maturity, the forecast volatility of the exchange rate, and other factors.

Time value is not *linear*. A one-year option is not valued at twice the value of a six-month option. An "at-the-money" option has greater time value than an "in-the-money" or "out-of-the-money" option. Accordingly, options—unlike forwards and futures—have *convexity*; that is, the change in the value of an option for a given change in the price of the underlying asset does not remain constant. This makes pricing options much more complex than pricing other foreign exchange instruments.

A major advance in the general theory of options pricing was introduced by Professors Black and Scholes in 1973. Their work, which was subsequently adapted for foreign exchange options, showed that under certain restrictive assumptions, the value of a European option on an underlying currency depends on six factors: 1) the spot exchange rate; 2) the interest rate on the base (or underlying) currency; 3) the interest rate on the terms currency; 4) the strike price at which the option can be exercised; 5) the time to expiration; and 6) the volatility of the exchange rate.

Volatility, a statistical measure of the tendency of a market price—in this case, the spot exchange rate—to vary over time, is the *only* one of these variables that is not known in advance, and is critically important in valuing and pricing options. Volatility is the annualized percentage change in an exchange rate, in terms of standard deviation (which is the most widely used statistical measurement of variation about a mean). The greater the forecast volatility, the greater the expected future movement potential in the exchange rate during the life of the option—i.e., the higher the likelihood the option will move "in-the-money," and so, the greater the value (and the cost) of the option, be it a put or a call. (With zero volatility, the option should cost nothing.)

If the one-year forward dollar-Swiss franc exchange rate is CHF 1.6000 = $1, and the volatility of a one-year European option price is forecast at 10 percent, there is implied the expectation, with a 68 percent probability, that one year hence, the exchange rate will be within CHF 1.6000 per dollar plus or minus 10 percent—that is, between CHF 1.4400 and CHF 1.7600 per dollar.

There are different measurements of volatility:

▶ *Historical* volatility is the actual volatility, or variance, of an exchange rate that occurred during some defined past time frame. This can be used as an indication or guide to future movements in the exchange rate.

▶ *Future* volatility is the expected variance in the exchange rate over the life of the option, and must be forecast.

▶ *Implied* volatility is the variance in an exchange rate that is implied by or built into the present market price of an option—thus, it is the market's current estimate of future movement potential as determined by supply and demand for the option in the market.

Implied volatility is a critical factor in options pricing. In trading options in the OTC interbank market, dealers express their quotes and execute their deals in terms of implied volatility. It is the metric, or measuring rod—dealers *think* and *trade* in terms of implied volatilities and *make their predictions* in that framework, rather than in terms of options *prices* expressed in units of a currency (which can change for reasons other than volatility changes—e.g., interest rates). It is easier to compare the prices of different options, or compare changes in market prices of an option over time, by focusing on implied volatility and quoting prices in terms of volatility. (For similar reasons, traders in outright forwards deal in terms of discounts and premiums from spot, rather than in terms of actual forward exchange rates.)

If market quotes and trades are to be made in terms of implied volatilities (or vols), all traders must use the same concept and conventions for computing volatility, so that they are all speaking the same language. The technique used in the market is to solve the Black-Scholes formula backwards—to take the price of an option in the market as given and calculate the volatility that is implied by that market price. Traders use this Black-Scholes-based computation of implied volatility as a way of communicating and understanding each other, even though they know that it has certain limitations. For example, they know (and take into account) that the technique inherently incorporates into the estimate of "implied volatility" all sources of mispricing, data errors, effects of bid-offer spreads, etc. They also know that the calculation assumes that all of the rigorous assumptions in the Black-Scholes theoretical pricing model apply, whereas in the market in which they are operating in the "real" world, these assumptions may not all apply.

Delta. Another important parameter for assessing options risk, also calculated from the Black- Scholes equation, is the *delta*, which measures how much the price of an option changes with a small (e.g., one percent) change in the value of the underlying currency.

Very importantly, the delta is also the *hedge ratio*, because it tells an option writer or a holder at any particular moment just how much spot foreign exchange he must be long or short to hedge an option position and eliminate (at least for that moment) the spot position risk.

Thus, if a trader *sold* a European call option on marks/put option on dollars with the face amount of $10 million, with the strike price set at the forward rate (an "at-the-money forward"), the chances *at that moment* are about 50-50 that the option will rise in value and at expiration be exercised, or fall in value and at expiration be worthless. If the option at that moment had a delta of 0.50, the trader could hedge, or neutralize, his option risk by taking an opposite spot position (purchase of marks/sale of dollars) equal to 50 percent of the option's face amount, or $5 million. This is called a "delta hedge." (If the strike price were "in-the-money," the delta would be between 0.50 and 1.00; if the strike price were "out-of-the-money," the delta would be between 0 and 0.50. At expiration, delta ends up either 0 (out-of-the-money and won't be exercised), or 1.00 (in the money and will be exercised).

Most option traders routinely "delta hedge" each option they purchase or write, buying or selling in the spot or forward market an amount that will fully hedge their initial exchange rate risk. Subsequently, as the exchange rate moves up or down, the option dealer will consider whether to maintain a neutral hedge by increasing or reducing this initial position in the spot or forward market.

However, the delta, or hedge ratio, whether it starts out at 0.50 or at some other number, will change continually, not only with each significant change in the exchange rate, but also with changes in volatility, or changes in interest rates, and, very importantly, delta will change with the passage of time. An option with a longer time to run is more valuable than an option with a shorter time to run. Thus, new calculations will continually be required as conditions change, to determine the new delta and the change in spot or forward foreign exchange position needed to maintain a neutral hedge position.

BOX 5-5

Delta Hedging

Option dealers who are actively trading in the market usually enter into an initial hedge (delta hedge) for each option each time they buy or write a put or a call.

Thus, if the delta is 0.50, the writer (seller) of a GBP 10 million *call* option might buy GBP 5 million spot and the buyer of the option sell GBP 5 million, as part of the option transaction.

At that point, *both* parties are hedged—the values of their option positions are exactly the same as the values of their spot hedges, but in opposite directions. Thus, if the price of the underlying currency moves up or down *by a very small amount* (say less than 1%), the option writer (and the option buyer) will gain or lose from the value of his spot hedge position an amount which would approximately *offset* the loss or gain in the value of the option.

However, the delta and the need for a spot hedge position change if the exchange rate changes and the option moves "into" or "out of" the money. If the price of the underlying currency moves up, and the value of the *call* option moves up, the delta moves up to, say, 0.60, so that to stay fully hedged the *writer* of the option has to *buy* more spot GBP, and the *buyer* of the option has to *sell* more spot GBP.

Option dealers have to keep a very close eye on exchange rate movements and decide, with each significant move up or down, whether to adjust delta hedges. In very choppy markets, it can be very expensive to delta hedge every movement up or down. For example, if a dealer wrote an option and the exchange rate bounced up and down (that is, had high volatility) so that the delta moved numerous times during the life of the option between, say, 0.45 and 0.55, the dealer could spend far more for hedging than for the premium that he received for writing the option—and incur a large overall loss even though the option might end up "out-of-the-money" and not be exercised.

Whether the option would result in a net gain or net loss for the option writer, assuming every exchange rate were delta hedged efficiently, would depend on whether the writer correctly forecast the *volatility* of the underlying currency, and priced the option on the basis of that volatility.

If the actual volatility of the currency over the life of the option turned out to be *exactly* the same as the volatility used in calculating the original premium, the delta hedge losses would (in principle) equal the original premium received, and the option writer would break even. If actual volatility turned out to be greater than forecast, the option writer would lose; if actual volatility were less than forecast, the option writer would gain. (This is not a surprising outcome, since an option is a bet on volatility—greater-than-anticipated volatility is beneficial to an option holder, and harmful to an option writer; less-than-anticipated volatility is the other way around.)

Delta hedging is a very important feature of the currency options market. It allows an important element of options risk to be transferred to the much larger and more liquid spot market, and thus allows options traders to quote a much broader range of options, and to quote narrower margins.

▶ Put-Call Parity

"Put-call parity" says that the price of a European *put* (or call) option can be deduced from the price of a European *call* (or put) option on the same currency, with the same strike price and expiration. When the strike price is the *same* as the forward rate (an "at-the-money" forward), the put and the call will be *equal* in value. When the strike price is *not* the same as the forward price, the *difference* between the value of the put and the value of the call will equal the *difference* in the present values of the two currencies.

Arbitrage assures this result. If the "put-call parity" relationship did *not* hold, it would pay to create *synthetic* puts or calls and gain an arbitrage profit. If, for example, an "at-the-money forward" call option were priced in the market at *more than* (rather than equal to) an "at-the-money forward" put option for a particular currency, a *synthetic* call option could be created at a cheaper price (by buying a put at the lower price and buying a forward at the market price). Other synthetics can be produced by other combinations (e.g., buying a call and selling a forward to produce a *synthetic put*; buying a call and selling a put to create a *synthetic long forward*; or selling a call and buying a put to create a *synthetic short forward*).

The "put-call parity" is very useful to options traders. If, for example, puts for a particular currency are being traded, but there are no market quotes for the corresponding call, traders can deduce an approximate market price for the corresponding call.

▶ How Currency Options are Traded

The OTC options market has become a 24-hour market, much like the spot and forward markets, and has developed its own practices and conventions. Virtually all of the major foreign exchange dealer institutions participate as market makers and traders. They try to stay fully abreast

of developments, running global options books that they may pass from one major center to another every eight hours, moving in and out of various positions in different markets as opportunities arise. Some major dealers offer options on large numbers of currency pairs (fifty or more), and are flexible in tailoring amounts and maturities (from same day to several years ahead). They can provide a wide array of different structures and features to meet customer wishes.

A professional in the OTC interbank options market asking another professional for a quote must specify more parameters than when asking for, say, a spot quote. The currency pair, the type of option, the strike price, the expiration date, and the face amount must be indicated. Dealers can do business with each other directly, by telephone or (increasingly) via electronic dealing system, which makes possible a two-way recorded conversation on a computer screen. Also, they can deal through an OTC (voice) broker. Among these dealers and brokers, quotes are presented in terms of the *implied volatility* of the option being traded.

As in other foreign exchange markets, a market maker is expected to give both a *bid*— the volatility at which he is prepared to *buy* an option of the specified features—and an *offer*— the volatility at which he is prepared to *sell* such an option.

For example, an interbank dealer, Jack from Bank X, might contact a market maker, Jill from Bank Z, identify himself and his institution and ask for a quote:

▶ Jack: "Three month 50-delta dollar put/yen call on 20 dollars, please."
 Jill: "14.50-15."
▶ Jack: "Yours at 14.50."
 Jill: "Done. I buy European three-month 50-delta dollar put/yen call on 20 dollars."

After this commitment to the trade, details ("deets") would then be worked out and agreed upon with respect to the exact expiration date, the precise spot rate, the exact strike price, and option premium. Customarily, in trades between dealers, there would be an offsetting transaction in spot or forward trade, in the opposite direction to the option, to provide both parties with the initial delta hedge.

Note that Jack and Jill specified *both* currencies—"dollar put/yen call." In foreign exchange options, since a call allowing you to buy yen for dollars at a certain price is also a put allowing you to sell dollars for yen at that price, it helps to avoid confusion if *both* formulations are mentioned.

▶ **Options Combinations and Strategies**

Combinations of options are used among the professionals for many purposes, including taking *directional* views on currencies—anticipating that a particular currency will move up or down—as well as taking *volatility* views on currencies—anticipating that a particular exchange rate will vary by more or by less than the market expects. Among the options combinations that are currently most widely used by traders in the OTC market are the following:

▶ A *straddle* consists of one put and one call with the same expiration date, face amount, and strike price. The strike price is usually set *at* the forward rate—or "at-the-money forward" (ATMF)—where the delta is about 0.50. A long straddle gains if there is higher than forecast volatility, regardless of which of the two currencies in the pair goes up and which goes down—and any potential loss is limited to the cost of the two premiums. By the same token, a short straddle gains if there is less than expected volatility, and the potential gain is limited to the premiums. Thus, a trader buys volatility by

buying a straddle, and sells volatility by selling a straddle. Straddles account for the largest volume of transactions in interbank trading.

▶ A *strangle* differs from a straddle in that it consists of a put and a call at *different* strike prices, both of which are "out-of-the-money," rather than "at-the-money." Often the strike prices are set at 0.25 delta. It is a less aggressive position than the straddle—a long strangle costs less to buy, but it requires a higher volatility (relative to market expectations of volatility) to be profitable.

▶ A *risk reversal* is a directional play, rather than a volatility play. A dealer exchanges an out-of-the-money (OTM) put for an OTM call (or vice versa) with a counterparty. Since the OTM put and the OTM call will usually be of different values, the dealer pays or receives a premium for making the exchange. The dealer will quote the implied volatility differential at which he is prepared to a make the exchange. If, for example, market expectations that the dollar will fall sharply against the Swiss franc are much greater than market expectations that the dollar will rise sharply against the Swiss franc, the dealer might quote the price of dollar-swissie risk reversals as follows: "For a three-month 0.25-delta risk reversal, 0.6 at 1.4 swissie calls over." That means the dealer is willing to *pay* a net premium of 0.6 vols (above the current implied ATM volatility) to buy a 0.25-delta OTM Swiss franc call and sell a 0.25-delta OTM Swiss franc put against the dollar, and he wants to *earn* a net premium of 1.4 vols (above the current implied ATM premium) for the opposite transaction. The holder of a risk reversal who has sold an OTM put and bought an OTM call will gain if the call is exercised, and he will lose if the put is exercised—but unlike the holder of a long straddle or long strangle (where the maximum loss is the premium paid), on the put he has sold his potential loss is unbounded.

CHART 5-4

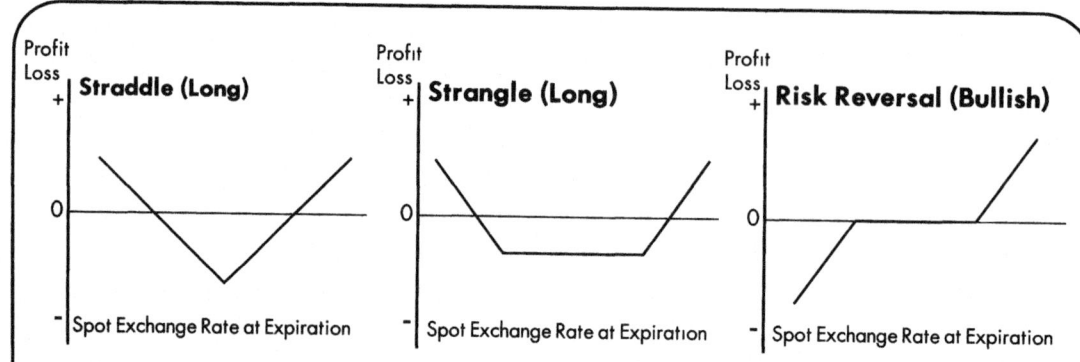

Straddle (Long) — Profit Loss / Spot Exchange Rate at Expiration

Strangle (Long) — Profit Loss / Spot Exchange Rate at Expiration

Risk Reversal (Bullish) — Profit Loss / Spot Exchange Rate at Expiration

Note: These figures show the payoff at expiration of various option combinations The left hand panel shows the combination of a purchased call and a purchased put, both at the same strike The middle panel shows a purchased call and a purchased put, where the strike price of the call is higher than the put's strike price The right hand panel depicts a purchased call and a sold put, where the call has a higher strike price

BOX 5-6

FOREIGN EXCHANGE OPTIONS GALORE

The array of foreign exchange options available in the OTC market to dealers and the broader market of customers is almost endless, and new forms are being created all the time. Naturally, the following list is not comprehensive.

▶ *Multi-currency options* give the right to exchange one currency, say dollars, for one of a number of foreign currencies at specified rates of exchange.

▶ *Split fee options* enable the purchaser to pay a premium up front, and a "back fee" in the future to obtain the foreign currency if the exchange rate moves in favor of the option.

▶ *Contingent options* involve a payoff that depends, not only on the exchange rate, but also on such conditions as whether the firm buying the option obtains the contract for which it is tendering, and for which the option was needed.

▶ There are a large number of options with *reduced or zero cash outlay* up front—which is made possible by combinations (buying one or more options and selling others) that result in a small or zero net initial outlay. One example is the *range forward* or *cylinder option*, which gives the buyer assurance that not more than an agreed maximum rate will be paid for needed foreign currency, but requires that the buyer agree he will pay no less than a stipulated (lower) minimum rate. Another example is the *conditional forward*, in which the premium is paid in the future but only if the exchange rate is below a specified level. A third example is the *participating forward*, in which the buyer is fully protected against a rise in the exchange rate, but pays a proportion of any decrease in the exchange rate. Such options—and there are any number of varieties—are popular since the buyer pays for his option by providing another option, rather than by paying cash, giving the *appearance* (which can be misleading) of cost-free protection, or the proverbial free lunch.

▶ There is the *all-or-nothing*, or *binary*, *option*, where, if the exchange rate is beyond the strike price at expiration, there is a fixed payout, and the amount is not affected by the magnitude of the difference between the underlying and the strike price.

▶ There are various forms of *path dependent* options, in which the option's value is determined, not simply by the exchange rate at the expiration of the option, but partly or exclusively by the path that the exchange rate took in arriving there. There are *barrier options*, in which, for example, the option expires worthless if the exchange rate hits some pre-agreed level, or, alternatively, in which the option pays off only if some pre-specified exchange rate is reached prior to expiration. There are *Bermuda* options (somewhere between American and European options) in which rights are exercisable on certain specified dates. There are Asian, or average rate, options, which pay off at maturity on the difference between the strike price and the average exchange rate over the life of the contract. There are look back options, or "no regrets" options, which give the holder the retroactive right to buy (sell) the underlying at its minimum (maximum) within the look back period. There are down-and-out options, knock-out options, and kick-out options, that expire if the market price of the underlying drops below a predetermined (out strike) price, and down-and-in options etc., that take effect only if the underlying drops to a predetermined (in strike) price.

▶ *Compound* options are options on options, and *chooser* options allow the holder to select before a certain date whether the option will be a put or a call.

▶ There are *non-deliverable currency options* (as there are non-deliverable forwards) which do not provide for physical delivery of the underlying currency when the option is exercised. If exercised, the option seller pays the holder the "in the money" amount on the settlement date in dollars or other agreed settlement currency.

▶ Other permutations include models developed in-house by the major dealers to meet individual customers' needs, and any number of customized arrangements that attach or embed options as part of more complex transactions.

FIGURE 5-1

MAIN CONTRACTS IN THE U.S. FOREIGN EXCHANGE MARKET

CONTRACTS	DESCRIPTION
Over-the-Counter Instruments	
A. *Outright Contracts*	Straightforward exchanges with various settlement dates
1. Spot	Settles two business days after deal date (or day 3) except Canada
Cash	Settles on deal date (or day 1)

(continued on page 56)

(continued from page 55)

Main Contracts in the U.S. Foreign Exchange Market

Value Tomorrow	Settles one business day after deal date (day 2)
2. Outright Forward	Settles on any pre-arranged date three or more business days after deal date (day 4 or beyond)

B. *FX Swap Contracts*	Exchange of principal with subsequent re-exchange at pre-agreed rate on pre-arranged date
▶ Short-Dated FX Swaps	Re-exchange in less than one month
1. Spot-Next	Arranged 2 days before spot value date; (or day 1); first leg settles on spot value date (or day 3); second leg settles next business day (or day 4)
2. Tom-Next	Arranged 1 day before spot value date; (or day 2); first leg settles on spot date (or day 3) second leg settles following business day (or day 4)
3. Spot-A-Week; (Spot-Two-Weeks)	Second leg settles same day one week later; (same day two weeks later)
▶ Forward FX Swaps	Re-exchange in one month or longer
1. Spot-Forward	First leg settles on spot date; second leg on a "straight" or standard forward date, e.g. 1, 2, 3, 6, 12 months
2. Odd-Date or Broken Date	First leg settles on spot date; second leg settles on a non-straight later date
3. Forward-Forward	First leg usually on a standard forward contract date; second leg a later standard forward contract date
4. Long Dates	First leg, spot date; second leg, a date beyond one year

C. Currency Swap Contracts	Initial exchange of principal (sometimes omitted), stream of interest payments, with subsequent re-exchange of principal on pre-arranged date

D. OTC Currency Option Contracts	Customized options; premium paid upfront; settlement two business days after exercise

Exchange-Traded Contracts

A. *Futures Contracts*	Standardized quarterly or other maturity dates; initial and maintenance margins with daily mark-to-market

B. *Exchange-Traded Currency Options Contracts*	
1. Options on Spot (Philadelphia)	On exercise, settlement in currency
2. Options on Futures (Chicago)	On exercise, settlement in futures position in currency

ALL ABOUT...

FIGURE 5-2

FOREIGN EXCHANGE

MONDAY, APRIL 27, 1998

Currency	Foreign Currency in Dollars Mon	Fri.	Dollars in Foreign Currency Mon	Fri	Currency	Foreign Currency in Dollars Mon.	Fri	Dollars in Foreign Currency Mon	Fri.
f-Argent (Peso)	1 0001	1 0001	9999	9999	Jordan (Dinar)	1 4134	1 4134	70751	70751
Australia (Dollar)	6467	6513	1 5463	1 5354	Lebanon (Pound)	000658	000658	1520 50	1520 50
Austria (Schilling)	0795	0792	12 577	12 620	Malaysia (Ringgit)	2635	2644	3 7950	3 7820
c-Belgium (Franc)	0270	0270	37 02	36 98	z-Mexico (Peso)	117385	117966	8 5190	8 4770
Brazil (Real)	8746	8749	1 1434	1 1430	Nethrlnd (Guilder)	4960	4942	2 0160	2 0234
Britain (Pound)	1 6742	1 6692	5973	5991	N Zealand (Dollar)	5539	5615	1 8054	1 7809
30-day fwd	1 6738	1 6640	5974	6010	Norway (Krone)	1340	1337	7 4601	7 4778
60-day fwd	1 6714	1 6591	5983	6027	Pakistan (Rupee)	0229	0229	43 64	43 68
90-day fwd	1 6670	1 6571	5999	6035	y-Peru (New Sol)	3551	3559	2 816	2 810
Canada (Dollar)	6949	6969	1 4390	1 4350	z-Philpins (Peso)	0256	0260	39 04	38 42
30-day fwd	6954	6970	1 4380	1 4347	Poland (Zloty)	2950	2933	3 39	3 41
60-day fwd	6958	6974	1 4371	1 4338	Portugal (Escudo)	005466	005428	182 94	184 24
90-day fwd	6962	6978	1 4364	1 4331	a-Russia (Ruble)	1631	1631	6 1310	6 1310
y-Chile (Peso)	002205	002215	453 55	451 45	Saudi Arab (Riyal)	2667	2666	3 7502	3 7505
China (Renminbi)	1208	1208	8 2784	8 2789	Singapore (Dollar)	6266	6289	1 5960	1 5900
Colombia (Peso)	000738	000737	1354 91	1355 94	SlovakRep (Koruna)	0289	0288	34 65	34 71
c-CzechRep (Koruna)	0302	0301	33 15	33 26	So Africa (Rand)	1982	1975	5 0455	5 0635
Denmark (Krone)	1462	1458	6 8386	6 8580	So Korea (Won)	000737	000732	1356 00	1367 00
Dominican (Peso)	0671	0676	14 90	14 80	Spain (Peseta)	006596	006549	151 61	152 70
ECU (ECU)	1 10310	1 09970	9065	9093	Sweden (Krona)	1298	1293	7 7032	7 7313
z-Ecudr (Sucre)	000200	000200	4995 00	4995 00	Switzerlnd (Franc)	6727	6708	1 4866	1 4907
d-Egypt (Pound)	2926	2926	3 4180	3 4180	30-day fwd	6761	6733	1 4790	1 4852
Finland (Mark)	1846	1830	5 4165	5 4630	60-day fwd	6786	6759	1 4736	1 4796
France (Franc)	1668	1666	5 9935	6 0010	90-day fwd	6810	6781	1 4685	1 4746
Germany (Mark)	5594	5588	1 7876	1 7895	Taiwan (Dollar)	0303	0303	33 04	32 99
30-day fwd	5609	5593	1 7828	1 7881	Thailand (Baht)	02574	02545	38 85	39 30
60-day fwd	5619	5603	1 7797	1 7849	Turkey (Lira)	000004	000004	247355 00	246535 00
90-day fwd	5628	5612	1 7768	1 7820	U A E (Dirham)	2723	2723	3 6728	3 6730
Greece (Drachma)	003181	003206	314 40	311 92	f-Uruguay (New Peso)	0971	0970	10 3000	10 3050
Hong Kong (Dollar)	1291	1290	7 7484	7 7497	Venzuel (Bolivar)	0019	0019	535 7000	535 0000
Hungary (Forint)	0048	0048	210 40	210 11					
y-India (Rupee)	0252	0252	39 680	39 690					
Indnsia (Rupiah)	000125	000124	8000 00	8050 00					
y-Iran (Rial)	000333	000333	3000 00	3000 00					
Ireland (Punt)	1 4128	1 4043	7078	7121					
Israel (Shekel)	2668	2674	3 7476	3 7403					
Italy (Lira)	000566	000565	1766 50	1770 00					
Japan (Yen)	007563	007624	132 23	131 16					
30-day fwd	007599	007668	131 59	130 41					
60-day fwd	007634	007701	131 00	129 86					
90-day fwd	007667	007733	130 43	129 31					

ECU European Currency Unit, a basket of European currencies The Federal Reserve Boards's index of the value of the dollar against 10 other currencies weighted on the basis of trade was 99 48 Monday, up 0 03 points or 0 03 percent from Friday's 99 45 A year ago the index was 97 04

a-Russian Central Bank rate

c-commercial rate, d-free market rate, f-financial rate, y-official rate, z-floating rate
Prices as of 3 00 p m Eastern Time from Dow Jones Telerate and other sources

CHAPTER 6

In addition to the instruments traded in the OTC market, the organized exchanges in Chicago, Philadelphia, and New York trade currency futures, and options on foreign currencies and on currency futures (Figure 6-1). This chapter describes exchange-traded futures and options

1. Exchange - Traded Futures

In the U.S. exchanges, a foreign exchange *futures* contract is an agreement between two parties to buy/sell a particular (non-U.S. dollar) currency at a particular price on a particular future date, as specified in a standardized contract common to all participants in that currency futures exchange. (See Box 6-1 on the evolution of foreign exchange futures.) When entering into a foreign exchange futures contract, no one is actually buying or selling anything—the participants are *agreeing* to buy or sell currencies on pre-agreed terms at a specified future date if the contract is allowed to reach maturity, which it rarely does.

A foreign exchange *futures* contract is conceptually similar to an outright *forward* foreign exchange contract, in that both are agreements to buy or sell a certain amount of a certain currency for another at a certain price on a certain date. However, there are important structural and institutional differences between the two instruments:

▶ Futures contracts are traded through public "open outcry" in organized, centralized exchanges that are regulated in the United States by the Commodity Futures Trading Commission. In contrast, forward contracts are traded "over-the-counter" in a market that is geographically dispersed, largely self-regulated, and subject to the ordinary laws of commercial contracts and taxation.

▶ Futures contracts are standardized in terms of the currencies that can be traded, the amounts, and maturity dates, and they are subject to the trading rules of the exchange with respect to daily price limits, etc. Forward contracts can be customized to meet particular customer needs.

▶ Futures contracts are "marked to market" and adjusted daily; there are initial and maintenance margins and daily cash settlements. Forward contracts do not require any cash payment until maturity (although a bank writing a forward contract may require collateral). Thus, a futures contract can be viewed as a portfolio or series of forwards, each covering a day or a longer period between cash settlements.

▶ Futures contracts are netted through the clearinghouse of the exchange, which receives the margin payments and guarantees the performance of both the buyer and the seller in every contract. Forward contracts are made directly between the two parties, with no clearinghouse between them.

The differences between the two instruments are very important. The fact that futures contracts are channeled through a clearinghouse and

FIGURE 6-1

Exchanges in the United States Trading FX Futures & Options

(Note-this table lists the FX futures and options contracts traded on the U.S. exchanges *before* the introduction of the euro in 1999. A number of the contracts will be changed when the euro is a traded currency).

Exchange and Contract	Face Value of Contract	1994 Volume of Contracts (000)
Chicago Mercantile Exchange (CME)		
Futures:		
Japanese Yen	¥12,500,000	6,613
Deutsche Mark	DEM125,000	10,956
DEM Rolling Spot	$250,000	127
French Franc	FRF500,000	49
Pound Sterling	£62,500	3,523
Pound Sterling		
Rolling Spot	$250,500	—
Canadian Dollar	CAN$100,000	1,740
Australian Dollar	$A100,000	355
Swiss Franc	SwF125,000	5,217
Cross Rate DEM	DEM125,000 x	
Japanese Yen	DEM/¥ Crossrate	—
Options on Futures:		
Yen Futures	(Same as Futures)	2,946
DEM Futures	(Same as Futures)	4,794
DEM Rolling Spot Futures	(Same as Futures)	—
FR Franc Futures	(Same as Futures)	1
Pound Sterling	(Same as Futures)	920
Pound Sterling		
Rolling Spot Futures	(Same as Futures)	—
Can. Dollar Futures	(Same as Futures)	186
Australian Dollar Futures	(Same as Futures)	8
Swiss Franc Futures	(Same as Futures)	768
Cross Rate DEM/Yen Futures	(Same as Futures)	—
Philadelphia Board of Trade		
Futures:		42
Australian Dollar	$A100,000	
Canadian Dollar	CAN$100,000	
Deutsche Mark	DEM125,000	
ECU	ECU125,000	
French Franc	F500,000	
Japanese Yen	¥12,500,000	
Pound Sterling	£62,500	
Swiss Franc	CHF125,000	

Exchange and Contract	Face Value of Contract	1994 Volume of Contracts (000)
Philadelphia Stock Exchange (PHLX)		
Options:		
Japanese Yen	¥6,250,000	999
Deutsche Mark	DEM62,500	3,445
French Franc	FR250,000	4,508
Pound Sterling	£31,250	411
Canadian Dollar	CAN$50,000	158
Australian Dollar	$A50,000	7
Swiss Franc	CHF62,500	428
ECU	ECU62,500	20
Cross Rate £/DEM	£31,250	28
Cross Rate DEM/¥	DEM62,500	33
Cash Settled DEM	DEM62,500	43
Customized Currency (Var. Underlying Currencies)		7
New York Board of Trade (FINEX Div.)		
Futures:		
U.S. Dollar Index	$1,000 x Index	558
ECU	ECU100,000	Not Traded
U.S. Dollar/DEM	DEM125,000	30
Cross Rate DEM/Yen	DEM125,000	31
Cross Rate DEM/F.Franc	DEM500,000	10
Cross Rate DEM/It.Lira	DEM25,000	4
Cross Rate £/DEM	£125,000	12
Options:		
U.S. Dollar Index	$1,000 x Index	42
Options on ECU Futures	ECU100,000	Not Traded
Mid-America Commodity Exchange (MIDAM)		
Futures:		
Japanese Yen	£6,250,000	68
Deutsche Mark	DEM62,500	11
Pound Sterling	£12,500	66
Canadian Dollar	CAN$50,000	10
Swiss Franc	CHF62,500	65

Source: International Capital Markets, Developments, Prospects, and Policy Issues. International Monetary Fund. Washington, D.C. August 1995, pp. 192-201.

BOX 6-1

DEVELOPMENT OF FOREIGN CURRENCY FUTURES

Foreign exchange futures—and *financial futures* generally—were introduced by the International Monetary Market (IMM) of the Chicago Mercantile Exchange in 1972, at the time of the breakdown of the Bretton Woods system of par value exchange rates. Prior to that time, there were organized exchange markets only for *commodity* futures, which first developed in the mid-1800s in the United States for trading in agricultural commodities such as wheat and pork bellies, imported foodstuffs such as coffee and cocoa, and industrial commodities such as copper and oil.

The IMM moved to apply the same organizational and trading techniques used in the commodity markets to a range of financial instruments, including foreign currency futures. This approach spread to other exchanges in the United States and abroad. A number of financial futures contracts are now traded, not only for currencies, but also for stock indexes and interest rates. In foreign exchange, the futures market now provides an alternative channel through which individual investors and businesses can take positions in foreign currencies for hedging or speculating.

In addition to the IMM of the Chicago Mercantile Exchange, the exchanges in the United States that trade foreign exchange futures are the Mid-America Commodity Exchange, which is a subsidiary of the Chicago Board of Trade; the Financial Instrument Exchange (Finex), which is a subsidiary of the New York Board of Trade (formerly Cotton Exchange); and the Philadelphia Board of Trade. In the United States, the Commodity Futures Trading Commission (CFTC) has jurisdiction over futures contracts, including foreign exchange futures.

The system of trading in futures markets is not greatly different from the practices introduced in the United States in the middle of the last century. There is a designated location (a "pit") where a large number of traders ("locals" who buy and sell for themselves, and "pit brokers" who also execute trades for others) communicate, often by hand signals, and complete their deals according to established rules, with all bids and offers announced publicly. Some new practices have been introduced. An "exchange for physicals" (EFP) market provides for trading futures contracts outside exchange hours, with prices for foreign exchange futures determined by interest parity from the spot market, which trades on a 24-hour day basis. Also, the Chicago Mercantile Exchange, working with others, has developed a system called "Globex" to provide for trading futures contracts when a futures exchange is closed.

"marked to market" daily means that credit risk is reduced. The fact that the clearinghouse is guaranteeing the performance of both sides also means that a contract can be canceled (or "killed") simply by buying a second contract that reverses the first and nets out the position. Thus, there is a good "secondary market." In a forward contract, if a holder wanted to close or reverse a position, there would have to be a second contract, and if the second contract is arranged with a different counterparty from the first, there would be two contracts and two counterparties, with credit risk on both.

Because of the differences in the two markets, it is not hard to understand why the two markets are used differently. Futures contracts seldom go to maturity—less than two percent result in delivery—and are widely used for purposes of financial hedging and speculation. The ease of liquidating positions in the futures market makes a futures contract attractive for those purposes. The high degree of standardization in the futures market means that traders need only discuss the number of contracts and the price, and transactions can be arranged quickly and efficiently.

Forward contracts are generally intended for delivery, and many market participants may need more flexibility in setting delivery dates than is provided by the foreign exchange futures market, with its standard quarterly delivery dates and its one-year maximum maturity. Transactions are typically for much larger amounts in the forward market —millions, sometimes many millions, of dollars—while most standardized futures contracts are each set at about $100,000 or less, though a single market participant can buy or sell multiple contracts, up to a limit imposed by the exchange. Also, forward contracts are not limited to the relatively small number of currencies traded on the futures exchanges.

The foreign currency futures market provides, to some extent, an alternative to the OTC forward market, but it also complements that market. Like the forward market, the currency futures market provides a mechanism whereby users can alter portfolio positions other than through the alternative of the cash or spot market. It can accommodate both short and long positions, and it can be used on a highly leveraged basis for both hedging and speculation. It thus facilitates the transfer of risk—from hedgers to speculators, or from speculators to other speculators.

In addition, the foreign currency futures market contributes to the "information" and the "price discovery" functions of markets— although the contribution may be moderate in the case of foreign exchange, since the estimated total turnover of currency futures markets is far below that of the market in outright forwards.

As in the case of forwards, prices in the foreign currency futures market are related to the spot market by *interest rate parity*. The theoretical price of a forward contract will be the spot exchange rate plus or minus the net cost of financing (the cost of carry), which is determined by the interest rate differential between the two currencies. In the case of futures, where there are margin requirements, daily marking to market, and different transactions costs, the price should presumably reflect those differences. In practice, however, the market prices of forwards and futures seem not to diverge very much for relatively short-term contracts.

▶ **Quotes for Foreign Currency Futures**
Figure 6-2 reports data from The New York Times, showing the foreign currency futures quotes on April 27, 1998—an arbitrarily chosen date—for contracts trading on the International Money Market (IMM) of the Chicago Mercantile Exchange; including the Japanese yen, the Deutsche mark, the Canadian dollar, the British pound, and the Swiss franc. (With the introduction of the euro in 1999, a number of the contracts will be changed.) Contracts for each currency are of a standard size—e.g., for the pound sterling the face amount is £62,500; for the Deutsche mark it is DEM 125,000. There are trading rules— for example, there is a minimum allowable price move between trades, and a maximum allowable price movement in a day. The

------ **FIGURE 6-2**

OTHER FUTURES

	Vol	High	Low	Settle	Net Chg	Lifetime High	Lifetime Low	Open Int
LIBOR 1-MONTH (CME) $3 million- pts of 100 pct								
May 98	3228	94 34	94 30	94 31	–	94 55	94 00	16869
30-DAY FED FUNDS (CBT) $5 million- pts of 100 pct								
Apr 98	971	94 53	94 52	94 53		94 74	94 18	4573
MUNICIPAL BONDS (CBT) $1000x index-pts & 32nds								
Jun 98	3355	120-31	119-27	120-02	– 1 18	125-19	119-27	23655
US DOLLAR INDEX (CTN) 1000 x index								
Jun 98	451	99 65	99 05	99 22	– 05	102 00	93 68	4575
CRB INDEX X 500 (NYFE) 500 x index								
Jun 98	65	226 40	224 80	226 20	+ 15	236 60	224 80	608
GSCI (Goldman $ Index) (CME) $250 X Nearby Index								
May 98	505	164 70	162 50	164 60	+ 40	192 80	159 30	25451
OATS (CBT) 5,000 bu minimum- cents per bushel								
May 98	427	124½	122	122	– 9¾	182½	122	2116
WINTER WHEAT (KC) 5,000 bu minimum- cents per bushel								
May 98	2975	318	314	317¼	– 1¾	411	333	7295
ROUGH RICE (CBT) 2,000 CWT- dollars per CWT								
May 98	169	10 140	10 090	10 110	– 030	11 690	9 640	1929
LUMBER (CME) 80,000 bd ft- $ per 1,000 bd ft								
May 98	560	302 40	296 00	297 00	– 4 00	370 00	291 70	1790
PALLADIUM (NYM) 100 troy oz- dollars per oz								
Jun 98	545	310 00	301 50	303 60	– 9 30	327 70	174 15	3824
BRITISH POUND (CME) 62,500 pounds, $ per pound								
Jun 98	6691	1 6740	1 6592	1 6702	+ 0062	1 6920	1 5656	37142
CANADIAN DOLLAR (CME) 100,000 dollars, $ per Cdn dlr								
Jun 98	5542	6986	6951	6956	– 0020	7453	6825	52131
GERMAN MARK (CME) 125,000 marks, $ per mark								
Jun 98	22557	5622	5577	5613	+ 0011	5981	5409	109245
JAPANESE YEN (CME) 12 5 million yen, $ per 100 yen								
Jun 98	15311	7697	7574	7615	– 0064	8746	7456	87335
SWISS FRANC (CME) 125,000 francs, $ per franc								
Jun 98	12419	6785	6712	6768	+ 0020	7304	6560	63240

Copyright © 1998 by the New York Times Co. Reprinted by permission.

delivery dates fall on the third Wednesday of the months of March, June, September, and December. The longest maturity is for one year.

Note that the futures exchange rates of all of the contracts are quoted in terms of the value of the foreign currency as measured in U.S. dollars, and premiums are quoted in U.S. cents per mark or pound—that is, in "direct" or "American" terms. This technique is consistent with long-standing practice in commodity exchanges for quoting futures contracts for agricultural and industrial products. But it differs from conventions in other parts of the exchange market—a Swiss franc forward would be priced at, say, "1.6000" (in CHF per dollar) while a Swiss franc future would be priced at the reciprocal, or "0.6250" (in dollars per CHF).

---

2. Exchange - Traded Currency Options

Exchange-traded currency options, like exchange-traded futures, utilize standardized contracts—with respect to the amount of the underlying currency, the exercise price, and the expiration date. Transactions are cleared through the clearinghouses of the exchanges on which they are traded, and the clearinghouses guarantee each party against default of the other. The option buyer—who has no further financial obligation after he has paid the premium—is not required to make margin payments. The option writer—who has all of the financial risk—is required to put up initial margin and to make additional (maintenance) margin payments if the market price moves adversely to his position.

In the United States, exchange-traded foreign exchange options were introduced in 1982. Options on foreign currencies presently are traded on the Philadelphia Stock Exchange (PHLX) and the Chicago Mercantile Exchange (CME). Options on a U.S. dollar index and on the ECU are traded on Finex, the financial division of the New York Cotton Exchange. The Securities and Exchange Commission (SEC) has jurisdiction over options on foreign currencies traded on national securities exchanges, while the Commodity Futures Trading Commission (CFTC) regulates options on foreign currency futures and options on foreign currencies traded on exchanges that are not securities exchanges. Abroad, options on foreign exchange are traded in various centers, including Singapore, Amsterdam, Paris, and Brussels.

The PHLX trades options contracts on *spot* foreign exchange for the Deutsche mark, Japanese yen, British pound, Australian dollar, Canadian dollar, French franc, Swiss franc, and ECU. (As with futures contracts, several of the options contracts will be changed when the euro is introduced.) The amounts of the foreign currencies per contract are set at one-half those in IMM futures contracts (e.g., a PHLX option contract on DEM is set at DEM 62,500 spot, or one-half of the IMM futures contract on DEM, which is DEM 125,000). Similarly, the expiration dates generally correspond to the March, June, September, and December maturity dates on IMM foreign exchange futures. The PHLX trades both American- and European-style options.

The CME trades options on the same eight currencies as the PHLX, but trades options on futures, rather than on spot, or cash. That is to say, at the CME a buyer can purchase a contract that provides the right, but not the obligation, for example, to go long on an exchange-traded foreign exchange futures contract at a strike price stated in terms of a different currency. If an option on foreign currency futures is exercised, any profit can be immediately recognized by closing out the futures position through an offsetting transaction.

All CME options on foreign exchange futures are American style—exercisable on or before the maturity date. These CME options contracts are the same size as IMM futures standardized contracts—each CME option represents the right to go long or short a single IMM foreign exchange futures contract. Figure 6-3 shows the quotes for call and put options on April 27, 1998.

---

3. Linkages

It is important to note how all of the main foreign exchange instruments described in Chapters 5 and 6 are linked to each other, creating a comprehensive network within which the forces of arbitrage can induce consistent rate relationships and pooled liquidity, which can benefit the various sectors of the market.

▶ *These linkages are summarized in Box 6-2.*

BOX 6-2

LINKAGES BETWEEN MAIN FOREIGN EXCHANGE INSTRUMENTS IN BOTH OTC AND EXCHANGE-TRADED MARKETS

▶ SPOT (settled two days after deal date, or T+2) = Benchmark price of a unit of the base currency expressed in a variable amount of the terms currency.

▶ Pre-Spot: *VALUE TOMORROW* (settled one day after deal date, or T+1) = Price based on spot rate adjusted for the value for one day of the interest rate differential between the two currencies. (Higher interest rate currency trades at a *premium* from spot.)

(continued on page 66)

(continued from page 65)

▶ Pre-Spot: CASH (settled on deal date, or T+0) = Price based on spot rate adjusted for the value for two days of the interest rate differential between the two currencies. (Higher interest rate currency trades at a premium from spot.)

▶ OUTRIGHT FORWARD = Price based on spot rate adjusted for the value of the interest rate differential between the two currencies for the number of days of the forward. (Higher interest rate currency trades at a forward *discount* from spot.)

▶ FX SWAP = One spot transaction plus one outright forward transaction for a given amount of the base currency, going in opposite directions, or else two outright forward transactions for a given amount of the base currency, with different maturity dates, going in opposite directions.

▶ CURRENCY FUTURES = Conceptually, a series of outright forwards, one covering each period from one day's marking to market and cash settlement to the next.

▶ CURRENCY SWAP = An exchange of principal in two different currencies at the beginning of the contract (sometimes omitted) and a re-exchange of same amount at the end; plus an exchange of two streams of interest payments covering each interest payment period, which is conceptually a series of outright forwards, one covering each interest payment period.

▶ CURRENCY OPTION = A *one-way* bet on the forward rate, at a price (premium) reflecting the market's forecast of the volatility of that rate. A synthetic forward position can be produced from a combination of options, and a package of options can be replicated by taking apart a forward.

FIGURE 6-3

OPTIONS ON FUTURES

FINANCIAL

EURODOLLARS (CME)
$1 million,pts of 100 pct

Strike	Calls			Puts		
Price	May	Jun	Sep	May	Jun	Sep
9400	r	0 22	0 23	r	0 01	0 10
9412	r	0 12	s	0 02	0 04	s
9425	0 03	0 05	0 09	0 07	0 09	0 21
9437	0 01	0 02	s	0 17	0 18	s
9450	r	0 01	0 04	0 29	0 30	0 40
9462	r	0 01	s	r	r	s

Prev call vol 38,262 Call open int 1,188,339
Prev put vol 52,060 Put open int 882,091

760	0 74	1 36	3 00	0 59	1.21	1 86
765	0.52	1 13	s	0.87	1 48	s
770	0 36	0 93	2 47	1 21	1 77	2 31
775	0 25	0 76	s	1 60	2 10	s

Prev call vol 4,057 Call open int 64,419
Prev put vol 3,565 Put open int 66,109

5 YR TREASURY (CBT)
$100,000, pts & 64ths of 100 pct

Strike	Calls			Puts		
Price	Jun	Sep	Dec	Jun	Sep	Dec
10700	r	r	s	-03	-24	s
10750	r	r	s	-08	-33	s
10800	-16	r	s	-15	-45	s
10832	r	r	s	r	s	s
10850	-20	-52	s	-29	-59	s
10900	-09	-39	s	-49	1-13	s

Prev call vol .3,753 Call open int.
Prev put vol .6,236 Put open int

10 YR. TREASURY (CBT)
$100,000 pnn, pts & 64ths of 100 pct

Strike	Calls			Puts		
Price	Jun	Sep	Dec	Jun	Sep	Dec
109	2-38	r	r	-03	-25	-45
109	s	s	r	s	s	r
110	1-43	r	r	-07	-40	1-00
111	-56	2-13	r	-21	-63	1-25
112	-23	1-08	1-30	-50	1-28	1-56
113	-07	-47	1-05	1-35	2-02	2-29

Prev call vol 13,868 Call open int
Prev put vol 0,000 Put open int

US TREASURY BONDS (CBT)
$100,000,pts & 64ths of 100 pct

Strike	Calls			Puts		
Price	Jun	Sep	Dec	Jun	Sep	Dec
116	2-62	3-45	r	-12	1-14	1-63
117	2-09	r	s	-23	1-02	s
118	1-27	2-33	3-01	-42	2-00	2-53
119	s	s	r	s	s	r
119	-56	r	r	1-06	1-46	2-51
120	-31	1-38	2-09	1-44	3-04	3-57

Prev call vol.39,961 Call open int
Prev put vol 45,859 Put open int

BRITISH POUND (CME)
62,500 pounds, cents per pound

Strike	Calls			Puts		
Price	May	Jun	Sep	May	Jun	Sep
1650	2 22	2 80	s	0 20	0 78	s
1660	1 44	2 14	3 40	0 42	1 12	3 00
1670	0 82	1 58	s	0 80	1 56	s
1680	0 46	1 14	2 48	1 44	2 12	4 06
1690	0 22	0 80	s	r	2 78	s
1700	0 12	0 56	1 76	r	3 52	r

Prev call vol 231 Call open int 12,590
Prev put vol 155 Put open int 12,172

GERMAN MARK (CME)
125,000 marks, cents per mark

Strike	Calls			Puts		
Price	May	Jun	Sep	May	Jun	Sep
550	1 20	1 40	2 09	0.07	0 28	0 71
555	0 80	1 06	s	0 17	0 43	s
560	0 46	0 78	1 47	0 33	0 65	1 07
565	0 24	0 56	s	0 61	0 93	s
570	0 14	0 38	1 01	r	1 24	1 59
575	0 08	0 26	s	r	r	s

Prev call vol .1,176 Call open int. 64,115
Prev put vol 926 Put open int 28,292

JAPANESE YEN (CME)
12,500,000 yen, cents per 100 yen

Strike	Calls			Puts		
Price	May	Jun	Sep	May	Jun	Sep
750	1 39	1 93	3 60	0 24	0 79	1 48
755	1 03	1 63	s	0 38	0 98	s

Copyright © 1998 by the New York Times Co. Reprinted by permission.

CHAPTER 7

In the discussion below, the focus is narrowed from the foreign exchange market as a whole to how a dealer institution operates within the market.

In the United States, each of the 93 institutions regarded as active dealers—the 82 commercial banks and 11 investment banks and other institutions surveyed by the Federal Reserve—is an important participant in the foreign exchange market. But there are major differences in the size, scope, and focus of their foreign exchange activities. Some are market makers; others are not. Some engage in a wide range of operations covering all areas of foreign exchange trading; others concentrate on particular niches or currencies. They vary in the extent and the nature of the trading they undertake for customers and for their own accounts.

The bulk of foreign exchange turnover is handled by a small number of the 93 active dealers. Ten institutions—about 11 percent of the total—account for 51 percent of foreign exchange turnover in the United States. In other countries, there is comparable concentration. In the U.K. market, the market share of the top ten institutions also was 50 percent.

The very largest dealers in the United States compete with each other, and there are major changes in rankings over time. Only six of the top ten firms in 1995 remained in the top 10 in 1998.

---

1. Trading Room Setup

In appearance, the trading rooms of many major dealer institutions are similar in many respects. All have rows of screens, computers, telephones, dedicated lines to customers and to brokers, electronic dealing and brokering systems, news services, analytic and informational sources, and other communications equipment. All have various traders specializing in individual currencies and cross-currencies, in spot, forwards, swaps, and options; their specialists in offshore deposit markets and various bond markets; and their marketing groups. There are funds managers and those responsible for proprietary transactions using the dealer's own funds. All have their affiliated "back offices"—not necessarily located nearby—where separate

staffs confirm transactions consummated by the traders and execute the financial payments and receipts associated with clearance and settlement. Increasingly, there are "mid-office" personnel, checking on the validity of valuations used by the traders and other matters of risk management.

The equipment and the technology are critical and expensive. For a bank with substantial trading activity, which can mean hundreds of individual traders and work stations to equip, a full renovation can cost many, many millions of dollars. And that equipment may not last long—with technology advancing rapidly, the state of the art gallops ahead, and technology becomes obsolete in a very few years. But in a business so dependent on timing, there is a willingness to pay for something new that promises information that is distributed faster or presented more effectively, as well as for better communications, improved analytical capability, and more reliable systems with better back-up. These costs can represent a significant share of trading revenue.

Each of the market-making institutions uses its facilities in its own way. All will consider it essential to have the most complete and most current information and the latest technology. But profits will depend, not just on having it, but on how that information and technology are used. Each institution will have its own business plan, strategy, approach, and objectives. Institutions will differ in scale of operations, segments of the market on which they wish to concentrate, target customers, style, and tolerance for risk.

The basic objectives and policy with respect to foreign exchange trading are set by senior management. They must decide which services the foreign exchange trading function will provide and how it will provide those services—often as part of a worldwide operation—in light of the bank's financial and human resources and its attitude toward risk. The senior management must determine, in short, the bank's fundamental business strategy—which includes, among other things, the emphasis to be placed on customer relationships and service vis-a-vis the bank's trading for its own account—and how that strategy will deal with changing market conditions and other factors.

The trading rooms are the trenches where the battle is joined, where each trader confronts the market, customers, competitors, and other players, and where each institution plays out its fundamental business strategy and sees it succeed or fail. A winning strategy and a sound battle plan are essential, and teamwork—with each trader being aware of the actions of others in the group and of developments in related markets—is of enormous importance to success.

---

2. The Diferent Kinds Of Trading Functions Of A Dealer Institution

A dealer bank or other institution is likely to be undertaking various kinds of foreign exchange trading—making markets, servicing customers, arranging proprietary transactions—and the emphasis on each will vary among institutions.

Market making is basic to foreign exchange trading in the OTC market. The willingness of market makers to quote both bids and offers for particular currencies, to take the opposite side to either buyers or sellers of the currency, facilitates trading and contributes to liquidity and price stability, and is considered important to the smooth and effective functioning of the market. An institution may choose to serve as a market maker purely because of the profits it believes it can earn on the spreads between buying and selling prices. But it may also see advantages in that the market-making function can broaden in an important way the range of banking services that the institution can offer to clients. In addition, it can give the market-making institution access to both market information and market liquidity that are valuable in its other activities.

Much of the activity in trading rooms is focused on marketing services and maintaining *customer relationships*. Customers may include treasurers of corporations and financial institutions; managers of investment funds, pension funds, and hedge funds, and high net worth individuals. A major activity of dealer institutions is managing customer business, including giving advice, suggesting strategies and ideas, and helping to carry out transactions and approaches that a particular customer may wish to undertake.

Dealers also trade foreign exchange as part of the bank's *proprietary* trading activities, where the firm's own capital is put at risk on various strategies. Whereas market making is usually reacting or responding to other people's requests for quotes, proprietary trading is proactive and involves taking an initiative.

Market making tends to be short-term and high volume, with traders focusing on earning a small spread from each transaction (or at least from most transactions)—with position-taking limited mainly to the management of working balances and reflecting views on very short-term forces and rate movements. A proprietary trader, on the other hand, is looking for a larger profit margin—in percentage points rather than basis points—based on a directional view about a currency, volatility, an interest rate that is about to change, a trend, or a major policy move—in fact, any strategic view about an opportunity, a vulnerability, or a mispricing in a market rate. Some dealers institutions—banks and otherwise—put sizeable amounts of their own capital at risk for extended periods in proprietary trading, and devote considerable resources to acquiring the risk analysis systems and other equipment and personnel to assist in developing and implementing such strategies. Others are much more limited in their proprietary trading.

---

3. Trading Among Major Dealers - Dealing Directly And Through Brokers

Dealer institutions trade with each other in two basic ways—*direct dealing* and through the *brokers market*. The mechanics of the two approaches are quite different, and both have been changed by technological advances in recent years.

▶ **Mechanics of Direct Dealing**
Each of the major market makers shows a running list of its main bid and offer rates—that is, the prices at which it will buy and sell the major currencies, spot and forward—and those rates are displayed to all market participants on

their computer screens. The dealer shows his prices for the base currency expressed in amounts of the terms currency. Both dollar rates and cross-rates are shown. Although the screens are updated regularly throughout the day, the rates are only *indicative*—to get a *firm* price, a trader or customer must contact the bank directly. In very active markets, quotes displayed on the screen can fail to keep up with actual market quotes. Also, the rates on the screen are typically those available to the largest customers and major players in the interbank market for the substantial amounts that the interbank market normally trades, while other customers may be given less advantageous rates.

A trader can contact a market maker to ask for a two-way quote for a particular currency. Until the mid-1980s, the contact was almost always by telephone—over dedicated lines connecting the major institutions with each other—or by telex. But *electronic dealing systems* are now commonly used—computers through which traders can communicate with each other, on a bilateral, or one-to-one basis, on screens, and make and record any deals that may be agreed upon. These electronic dealing systems now account for a very large portion of the direct dealing among dealers.

As an example of direct dealing, if trader Mike were asking market maker Hans to give quotes for buying and selling $10 million for Swiss francs, Mike could contact Hans by electronic dealing system or by telephone and ask rates on "spot dollar-swissie on ten dollars."

Hans might respond that "dollar-swissie is 1.4585-90;" or maybe "85-90 on 5," but more likely, just "85-90," if it can be assumed that the "big figure" (that is, 1.45) is understood and taken for granted. In any case, it means that Hans is willing to *buy* $10 million at the rate of CHF 1.4585 per dollar, and *sell* $10 million at the rate of CHF 1.4590 per dollar. Hans will provide his quotes within a few seconds and Mike will respond within a few seconds. In a fast-moving market, unless he responds promptly—in a matter of seconds—the market maker cannot be held to the quote he has presented. Also, the market maker can change or withdraw his quote at any time, provided he says "change" or "off" *before* his quote has been accepted by the counterparty.

It can all happen very quickly. Several conversations can be handled simultaneously on the dealing systems, and it is possible to complete a number of deals within a few minutes. When he hears the quotes, Mike will either buy, sell, or pass—there is no negotiation of the rate between the two traders. If Mike wants to buy $10 million at the rate of CHF 1.4590 per dollar (i.e., accept Hans' offer price), Mike will say "Mine" or "I buy" or some similar phrase. Hans will respond by saying something like "Done—I sell you ten dollars at 1.4590." Mike might finish up with "Agreed—so long."

Each trader then completes a "ticket" with the name and amount of the base currency, whether bought or sold, the name and city of the counterparty, the term currency name and amount, and other relevant information. The two tickets, formerly written on paper but now usually produced electronically, are promptly transmitted to the two "back offices" for confirmation and payment. For the two traders, it is one more deal completed, one of 200-300 each might complete that day. But each completed deal will affect the dealer's own limits, his bank's currency exposure, and perhaps his approach and quotes on the next deal.

The spread between the bid and offer price in this example is 5 basis points in CHF per dollar, or about three one-hundredths of one percent of the dollar value. The size of the spread will, other things being equal, tend to be comparable among currencies on a *percentage* basis, but larger in *absolute* numbers the lower the value of the currency unit—i.e., the spread in the dollar-lira rate will tend to be wider in *absolute number* (of lire) than the spread in dollar-swissie, since the dollar sells for a larger absolute number of lire than of Swiss francs. The width of the spread can also be affected by a large number of other factors—the amount of liquidity in the market, the size of the transaction, the number of players, the time of day, the volatility of market conditions, the trader's own position in that currency, and so forth. In the United States, spreads tend to be narrowest in the New York morning-Europe afternoon period, when the biggest markets are open and activity is heaviest, and widest in the late New York afternoon, when European and most large Asian markets are closed.

▶ **Mechanics of Trading Through Brokers: Voice Brokers and Electronic Brokering Systems**
The traditional role of a broker is to act as a go-between in foreign exchange deals, both within countries and across borders. Until the 1990s, all brokering in the OTC foreign exchange market was handled by what are now called live or *voice brokers*.

Communications with voice brokers are almost entirely via dedicated telephone lines between brokers and client banks. The broker's activity in a particular currency is usually broadcast over open speakers in the client banks, so that everyone can hear the rates being quoted and the prices being agreed to, although not specific amounts or the names of the parties involved.

A live broker will maintain close contact with many banks, and keep well informed about the prices individual institutions will quote, as well as the depth of the market, the latest rates where business was done, and other matters. When a customer calls, the broker will give the best price available (highest bid if the customer wants to sell and lowest offer if he wants to buy) among the quotes on both sides that he or she has been given by a broad selection of other client banks.

In direct dealing, when a trader calls a market maker, the market maker quotes a two-way price and the trader accepts the bid or accepts the offer or passes. In the voice brokers market, the dealers have additional alternatives. Thus, with a broker, a market maker can make a

quote for only one side of the market rather than for both sides. Also, a trader who is asking to see a quote may have the choice, not only to hit the bid or to take (or lift) the offer, but also to join either the bid or the offer in the brokers market, or to improve either the bid or the offer then being quoted in the brokers market.

At the time a trade is made through a broker, the trader does not know the name of the counterparty. Subsequently, credit limits are checked, and it may turn out that one dealer bank must refuse a counterparty name because of credit limitations. In that event, the broker will seek to arrange a name-switch—i.e., look for a mutually acceptable bank to act as intermediary between the two original counterparties. The broker should not act as principal.

Beginning in 1992, *electronic brokerage systems* (or *automated order-matching systems*) have been introduced into the OTC spot market and have gained a large share of some parts of that market. In these systems, trading is carried out through a network of linked computer terminals among the participating users. To use the system, a trader will key an order into his terminal, indicating the amount of a currency, the price, and an instruction to buy or sell. If the order can be filled from other orders outstanding, and it is the best price available in the system from counterparties acceptable to that trader's institution, the deal will be made. A large order may be matched with several small orders.

If a new order cannot be matched with outstanding orders, the new order will be entered into the system, and participants in the system from other banks will have access to it. Another player may accept the order by pressing a "buy" or "sell" button and a transmit button. There are other buttons to press for withdrawing orders and other actions.

Electronic brokering systems now handle a substantial share of trading activity. These systems are especially widely used for *small transactions* (less than $10 million) in the *spot market* for the most *widely traded currency pairs*—but they are used increasingly for larger transactions and in markets other than spot. The introduction of these systems has resulted in greater price transparency and increased efficiency for an important segment of the market. Quotes on these smaller transactions are fed continuously through the electronic brokering systems and are available to all participating institutions, large and small, which tends to keep broadcast spreads of major market makers very tight. At the same time electronic brokering can reduce incentives for dealers to provide two-way liquidity for other market participants. With traders using quotes from electronic brokers as the basis for prices to customers and other dealers, there may be less propensity to act as market maker. Large market makers report that they have reduced levels of first-line liquidity. If they need to execute a trade in a single sizeable amount, there may be fewer reciprocal counterparties to call on. Thus, market liquidity may be affected in various ways by electronic broking.

Proponents of electronic broking also claim there are benefits from the certainty and clarity of trade execution. For one thing there are clear *audit trails*, providing back offices with information enabling them to act quickly to reconcile trades or settle differences. Secondly, the electronic systems will match orders only between counterparties that have available *credit lines* with each other. This avoids the problem sometimes faced by voice brokers when a dealer cannot accept a counterparty he has been matched with, in which case the voice broker will need to arrange a "credit switch," and wash the credit risk by finding an

acceptable institution to act as intermediary. Further, there is greater certainty about the posted price and greater certainty that it can be traded on. Disputes can arise between voice brokers and traders when, for example, several dealers call in simultaneously to hit a given quote. These uncertainties are removed in an electronic process. But electronic broking does not eliminate all conflicts between banks. For example, since dealers typically type into the machine the last two decimal points (pips) of a currency quote, unless they pay close attention to the *full* display of the quote, they may be caught unaware when the "big figure" of a currency price has changed.

With the growth of electronic broking, voice brokers and other intermediaries have responded to the competitive pressures. Voice brokers have emphasized newer products and improved technology. London brokers have introduced a new automated confirmation system, designed to bring quick confirmations and sound audit trails. Others have emphasized newer products and improved technology. There have also been moves to focus on newer markets and market segments.

The two basic channels, direct dealing and brokers—either voice brokers or electronic broking systems—are complementary techniques, and dealers use them in tandem. A trader will use the method that seems better in the circumstances, and will take advantage of any opportunities that an approach may present at any particular time. The decision on whether to pay a fee and engage a broker will depend on a variety of factors related to the size of the order, the currency being traded, the condition of the market, the time available for the trade, whether the trader wishes to be seen in the market (through direct dealing) or wants to operate more discreetly (through brokers), and other considerations.

The 1998 Federal Reserve turnover survey indicated that brokers handled 41 percent of spot transactions, and a substantially smaller percentage of outright forwards and FX swaps. Altogether, 24 percent of total U.S. foreign exchange activity in the three traditional markets was handled by brokers. In the brokers market, 57 percent of turnover is now conducted through automated order-matching systems, or electronic brokering, compared with 18 percent in 1995.

4. Operations Of A Foreign Exchange Department

Typically the foreign exchange department of a bank will meet each morning, before trading starts, review overnight developments, receive reports from branches and affiliated outlets in markets that opened earlier, check outstanding orders from customers, discuss their views toward the market and the various currencies, and plan their approaches for the day. As market events unfold, they may have to adapt their view and modify their approach, and the decisions on whether, when, and how to do so can make the difference between success and failure.

Each institution has its own decision-making structure based on its own needs and resources. A chief dealer supervises the activities of individual traders and has primary responsibility for hiring and training new personnel. The chief dealer typically reports to a senior officer responsible for the bank's international asset and liability area, which includes, not only foreign exchange trading, but also Eurodollar and other offshore deposit markets, as well as derivatives activities intimately tied to foreign exchange trading. Reporting to the chief dealer are a number of traders specializing in one or more currencies. The most actively traded currencies are handled by the more senior traders, often assisted by a junior person who may also handle a less actively traded currency. But the actions of any trader, regardless of rank, commit the bank's funds. All need to be on their toes. Even a day trader whose objective may be simply to buy at his bid price and sell at his offer is in a better position to succeed if he is well informed, and can read the market well, see where rates may be headed, and understand the forces at play. He must have a clear understanding of his currency position, his day's net profit or loss, and whether and by how much to shade his quotes in one direction or the other.

Many senior traders have broad responsibility for the currencies they trade—quoting prices to customers and other dealers, dealing directly and with the brokers market, balancing daily payments and receipts by arranging swaps and other transactions, and informing and advising customers. They may have certain authority to take a view on short-term exchange rate and interest rate movements, resulting in a short or long position within authorized limits. The chief dealer is ultimately responsible for the profit or loss of the operation, and for ensuring that management limits to control risk are fully observed.

Most large market-making institutions have "customer dealers" or "marketers" in direct contact with corporations and other clients, advising customers on strategy and carrying out their instructions. This allows individual traders in spot, forwards, and other instruments to concentrate on making prices and managing positions. If the client deals, the marketer must make sure that all of the various traders involved in the transactions are informed of the particulars.

When a customer asks a market-making institution for the rates at which it is willing to buy and sell a particular currency, the response will be based on a number of factors. In deciding what bid and offer prices to quote, the trader takes into account the current quotations in the market, the rates at which the brokers are transacting business, the latest trends and expectations, whether the bank is long or short the currency in question, and views about where rates are headed. The trader is expected to be knowledgeable about both "fundamental" analysis (broad macroeconomic and financial trends underlying the supply and demand conditions for currencies that are being traded) and "technical" analysis (charts showing price patterns and volume trends). The trader also should be aware of the latest economic news, political developments, predictions of experts, and the technical position of the various currencies in the market. In bid and offer price quotes, the trader also may be influenced by the size of the trade—on the one hand, a small trade may call for a less favorable rate to cover fixed costs; on the other hand, a large trade may be much more difficult to offset.

When making quotes on outright forwards and FX swaps, in addition to understanding all the factors that may be influencing the spot rate, the trader must know the interbank swap rates for the currency in question—since the swap rate will reflect the interest rate differential between the two currencies being traded, and is the critical factor in determining the amount of premium or discount at which the forward exchange rate will trade. The trader, in addition, must be aware of the maturity structure of the contracts already outstanding in his bank's foreign exchange book, and whether the proposed new transaction would add to or reduce the mismatches. Of course, in offering a quote for an option, a trader must consider other

complex factors. The trader will have loaded into his computer various formulas for estimating the future volatility of the currency involved, along with spot and forward exchange rates and interest rates, so that he can very quickly calculate and quote the price of the premium when given the particulars of the transaction.

On top of all this, in setting quotes, a trader will take into account the relationship between the customer or counterparty and his institution. If it is a valued customer, the trader will want to consider the longer-term relationship with that customer and its importance to the longer-term profitability of the bank. Similarly, when dealing with another market maker institution, the trader will bear in mind the necessity of being competitive and also the benefit of relationships based on reciprocity.

When asked for a quote, the trader must respond immediately, making an instantaneous assessment of these thousand and one factors. Quotes have to be fine enough to attract customers and to win an appropriate share of the business—but also not too fine, since the trader wants to avoid excessive or inappropriate risk and to make profits. A trader wants to be an active participant in the market—it's helpful in keeping abreast of what's going on, and he wants others to think of him as a potential counterparty—but he doesn't want to "overtrade" or feel he must be in on every trade.

As the traders in a foreign exchange department buy and sell various currencies throughout the day in spot, forward, and FX swap transactions, the trading book or foreign exchange position of the institution changes, and long and short positions in individual currencies arise. Since every transaction involves an exchange of one currency for another, it results in two changes in the bank's book, creating a "long" (credit) position in one currency and a "short" (debit) position in another. The foreign exchange department must continuously keep track of the long and short positions in various currencies as well as how any positions are to be financed. The bank must know these positions precisely at all times, and it must be prepared to make the necessary payments on the settlement date.

Trading in the nontraditional instruments—most importantly, foreign exchange options—requires its own arrangements and dedicated personnel. Large options-trading institutions have specialized groups for handling different parts of the business: some personnel contact the customers, quote prices, and make deals; others concentrate on putting together the many pieces of particularly intricate transactions; and still others work on the complex issues of pricing, and of managing the institution's own book of outstanding options, written and held. A major options-trading institution needs, for its own protection, to keep itself aware, on a real time basis, of the status of its entire options portfolio, and of the risk to that portfolio of potential changes in exchange rates, interest rates, volatility of currencies, passage of time, and other risk factors. On the basis of such assessments, banks adapt options prices and trading strategy. They also follow the practice of "dynamically hedging" their portfolios—that is, continuously considering on the basis of formulas, judgment, and other factors, possible changes in their portfolios, and increases or reductions in the amounts they hold of the underlying instruments for hedging purposes, as conditions shift and expected gains or losses on their portfolios increase or diminish.

5. Back Office Payments And Settlements

Every time a deal to buy or sell foreign exchange is agreed upon by two traders in their trading rooms, a procedure is set in motion by which the "back offices" of the two institutions confirm the transaction and make the necessary funds transfers. The back office is usually separated physically from the trading room for reasons of internal control—but it can be next door or thousands of miles away.

For each transaction, the back office receives for processing the critical information with respect to the contract transmitted by the traders, the brokers, and the electronic systems. The back offices confirm with each other the deals agreed upon and the stated terms—a procedure that can be done by telephone, fax, or telex, but that is increasingly handled electronically by systems designed for this purpose. If there is a disagreement between the two banks on a relevant factor, there will be discussions to try to reach an understanding. Banks and other institutions regularly tape record all telephone conversations of traders. Also, electronic dealing systems and electronic broking systems automatically record their communications. These practices have greatly reduced the number of disputes over what has been agreed to by the two traders. In many cases, banks participate in various bilateral and multilateral netting arrangements with each other, instead of settling on the basis of each individual transaction. As discussed in Chapter 8, netting, by reducing the amounts of gross payments, can be both a cheaper and safer way of settling.

Payments instructions are promptly exchanged—in good time before settlement—indicating, for example, on a dollar-yen deal, the bank and account where the dollars are to be paid and the bank and account where the yen are to be paid. On the value date, the two banks or correspondent banks debit-credit the clearing accounts in response to the instructions received. Since 1977, an automated system known as SWIFT (Society for the Worldwide Interbank Financial Telecommunications) has been used by thousands of banks for transferring payment instructions written in a standardized format among banks with a significant foreign exchange business.

When the settlement date arrives, the yen balance is paid (for an individual transaction or as part of a larger netted transaction) into the designated account at a bank in Japan, and a settlement occurs there. On the U.S. side, the dollars are paid into the designated account at a bank in the United States, and the dollar settlement—or shift of dollars from one bank account to another—is made usually through CHIPS (Clearing House Interbank Payments System), the electronic payments system linking participating depository institutions in New York City.

After the settlements have been executed, the back offices confirm that payment has indeed been made. The process is completed. The individual, or institution, who wanted to sell dollars for yen has seen his dollar bank account decline and his bank account in yen increase; the other individual, or institution, who wanted to buy dollars for yen has seen his yen bank deposit decline and his dollar bank account increase.

CHAPTER 8

The foreign exchange business is by its nature risky, because it deals primarily in risk—

measuring it, pricing it, accepting it when appropriate, and managing it The success of

a bank or other institution trading in the foreign exchange market depends critically on

how well it assesses, prices, and manages risk, and on its ability to limit losses from

particular transactions and to keep its overall exposure controlled

Broadly speaking, the risks in trading foreign exchange are the same as those in marketing other financial products. These risks can be categorized and subdivided in any number of ways, depending on the particular focus desired and the degree of detail sought. Here, the focus is on two of the basic categories of risk—market risk and credit risk (including *settlement* risk and *sovereign* risk)—as they apply to foreign exchange trading. Note is also taken of some other important risks in foreign exchange trading—*liquidity* risk, *legal* risk, and *operational* risk.

1. Market Risk

Market risk, in simplest terms, is price risk, or "exposure to (adverse) price change." For a dealer in foreign exchange, two major elements of market risk are *exchange rate risk* and *interest rate risk*—that is, risks of adverse change in a currency rate or in an interest rate.

Exchange rate risk is inherent in foreign exchange trading. A trader in the normal course of business—as he buys or sells foreign currency to a customer or to another bank—is creating an "open" or "uncovered" position (long or short) for his bank in that currency, unless he is covering or transferring out of some previous position. Every time a dealer takes a new foreign exchange position—in spot, outright forwards, currency futures, or currency options—that position is immediately exposed to the risk that the exchange rate may move against it, and the dealer remains exposed until the transaction is hedged or covered by an offsetting transaction. The risk is continuous—and a gap of a few moments or less can be long enough to see what was thought to be a profitable transaction changed to a costly loss.

Interest rate risk arises when there is any mismatching or gap in the maturity structure. Thus, an uncovered outright forward position can change in value, not only because of a change in the spot rate (foreign exchange risk), but also because of a change in interest rates (interest rate risk), since a forward rate reflects the interest rate differential between the two currencies. In an FX swap, there is no shift in foreign exchange exposure, and the market risk is interest rate risk. In addition to FX swaps and currency swaps, outright forwards, currency futures, and currency options are all subject to interest rate risk.

There are *two forms* of market risk—an adverse change in *absolute* prices, and an adverse change in *relative* prices. With respect to relative price changes, "basis risk" is the possibility of loss from using, for example, a U.S. dollar position to offset Argentine currency exposure (in the expectation that the Argentine currency will move in step with the U.S. dollars), and then seeing the Argentine currency fail to maintain the relationship with the U.S. dollar that had been expected. It can also occur if a short-term interest rate that was used to offset a longer-term interest rate exposure fails to maintain the expected relationship because of a shift in the yield curve. To limit basis risk, traders try to stay well informed of statistical correlations and co-variances among currencies, as well as likely yield curve trends.

▶ Measuring and Managing Market Risk

Various mechanisms are used to control market risk, and each institution will have its own system. At the most basic trading room level, banks have long maintained clearly established *volume* or *position limits* on the maximum open position that each trader or group can carry overnight, with separate—probably less restrictive—intraday or "daylight" limits on the maximum open position that can be taken during the course of a trading session. These limits are carefully and closely monitored, and authority to exceed them, even temporarily, requires approval of a senior officer.

But volume limits alone are not enough. A $10 million open position in a very volatile currency represents a much bigger risk to profits than $10 million exposure in a relatively stable currency. Banks and other firms dealing in foreign exchange put limits, not only on the overall volume of their foreign exchange position, but also on their *estimated potential losses* during, say, the next 24 hours, which they

estimate through calculations of "value at risk" (VAR), "daily earnings at risk" (DEAR), or other dollars-at-risk measurements. Thus, a trading unit might have an overnight volume limit of say, $10 million, and also a VAR limit of, say, $150,000.

▶ Value at Risk

The rapid growth of derivatives in recent years—growth both in the amounts traded and in the innovative new products developed—has introduced major new complexities into the problem of measuring market risk. Banks and other institutions have seen the need for new and more sophisticated techniques adapted to the changed market situation.

Consider, for example, the question of the valuation of derivatives. If a trader entered into a contract for the forward purchase of $10 million of pounds sterling six months hence at today's 6-month forward price for GBP, the *notional* or face value of the contract would be $10 million. The *market* value (gross replacement value) of the contract would at the outset be zero—but that market value could change very abruptly and by significant amounts. Neither the notional value of that forward contract nor the snapshot of the market value as of a particular moment provides a very precise and comprehensive reflection of the risk, or potential loss, to the trader's book. For currency options, the problem is much more complex—the value of an option is determined by a number of different elements of market risk, and values can change quickly, moving in a non-linear fashion. Market participants need a more *dynamic* way of assessing market risk as it evolves over time, rather than measuring risk on the basis of a *snapshot* as of one particular moment, or by looking at the *notional* amounts of funds involved.

In a report of the Group of Thirty entitled *Derivatives: Practices and Principles*, industry members recommended a series of actions to assist in the measurement of market risk. They recommended that institutions adopt a "value at risk" (VAR) measure of market risk, a technique that can be applied to foreign exchange and to other products. It is used to assess not only the market risk of the foreign exchange position of the trading room, but also the broader market risk inherent in the foreign exchange position resulting from the totality of the bank or firm's activities.

VAR estimates the potential loss from market risk across an entire portfolio, using probability concepts. It seeks to identify the fundamental risks that the portfolio contains, so that the portfolio can be decomposed into underlying risk factors that can be quantified and managed. Employing standard statistical techniques widely used in other fields, and based in part on past experience, VAR can be used to estimate the *daily statistical variance*, or standard deviation, or volatility, of the entire portfolio. On the basis of that estimate of variance, it is possible to estimate the expected loss from adverse price movements with a specified probability over a particular period of time (usually a day).

Thus, a bank might want to calculate the maximum estimated loss in its foreign exchange portfolio in one day from market risk on the basis of, say, a 97.5 confidence interval. It could then calculate that on 39 days out of 40 days, the expected loss from market risk (adverse price changes) would be no greater than "x."

VAR is regarded by market participants as helpful to an institution in assessing its market risk and providing a more comprehensive picture than is otherwise available. The institution can use the calculations as a framework for considering other questions—e.g., what steps, if any, should be taken to hedge or adjust the book, how does the situation look in terms of the institution's strategy and tolerance for risk, and other management issues.

However, VAR has limitations. It provides an *estimate*, not a *measurement*, of potential loss. It does not predict by *how much* the loss will exceed that amount in the one day in forty (or other selected probability) when the estimated loss will exceed the specified amount of VAR. The calculations are based on historical experience and other forecasts of volatility, and are valid only to the extent that the assumptions are valid. In using past experience, there are always questions of whether the past will be prologue, which period of past experience is most relevant, and how it should be used. Many alternative approaches are possible: Should the formula be weighted toward the recent past? Should a more extensive period of history be covered? Should judgments about the fundamental condition of the market be introduced?

Also, there are certain statistical limitations. VAR calculations use standard deviation measurements—the familiar bell-shaped curve, which reflects a "normal" distribution. But there is empirical evidence that daily *exchange rate changes* usually do not closely fit a normal distribution; they exhibit a property called "leptokurtosis," which means they have "fatter tails" (more outliers) and a higher mid-range than is seen in a normal distribution. Some practitioners make adjustments (e.g., they look toward a 97.5%, or 99%, rather than a 95%, confidence level) in light of these uncertainties.

Despite its limitations, VAR is increasingly used by market participants, along with risk limits, monitoring, stress scenarios, and other techniques to assess market risk. They regard it as a considerable complement to and improvement over previous approaches, providing a dynamic assessment of probabilities, rather than a snapshot approach. Undoubtedly, with experience, new adjustments and variations will appear. In all likelihood, the procedures will become increasingly sophisticated with increasing focus on the *extent* of expected future loss, in addition to the *probability*.

Indeed, in calculating risk-based capital requirements, the bank supervisors of the G-10 major industrial nations, acting through the Basle Committee on Bank Supervision, now allow large banking institutions with major trading activities in foreign exchange and other instruments to measure their market risk through their internal value-at-risk models. Thus, each institution can use its own internal model as the framework for making its calculations of its market risk-based capital requirement—but subject to the approval of the appropriate supervisor, and to conformity with certain minimum qualitative and quantitative standards regarding measurement and management of market risk.

2. Credit Risk

Credit risk, inherent in all banking activities, arises from the possibility that the counterparty to a contract cannot or will not make the agreed payment at maturity. When an institution provides credit, whatever the form, it expects to be repaid. When a bank or other dealing institution enters a foreign exchange contract, it faces a risk that the counterparty will not perform according to the provisions of the contract. Between the time of the deal and the time of the settlement, be it a matter of hours, days, or months, there is an extension of credit by both parties and an acceptance of credit risk by the banks or other financial institutions involved. As in the case of market risk, credit risk is one of the fundamental risks to be monitored and controlled in foreign exchange trading.

In banking, the reasons a counterparty may be unwilling or unable to fulfill its contractual obligations are manifold. There are cases when a corporate customer enters bankruptcy, or a bank counterparty becomes insolvent, or

foreign exchange or other controls imposed by governmental authorities prohibit payment.

If a counterparty fails before the trade falls due for settlement (pre-settlement risk), the bank's position is unbalanced and the bank is exposed to loss for any changes in the exchange rate that have occurred since the contract was originated. To restore its position, the bank will need to arrange a new transaction, and very likely at an adverse exchange rate, since no one defaults on a contract that yields positive gains. In situations of bankruptcy, a trustee for the bankrupt company will endeavor to "cherry pick," or perform according to the terms on those contracts that are advantageous to the bankrupt party, while disclaiming those that are disadvantageous.

In foreign exchange trading, banks have long been accustomed to dealing with the broad and pervasive problem of credit risk. "Know your customer" is a cardinal rule and credit limits or dealing limits are set for each counterparty—presumably after careful study of the counterparty's creditworthiness—and adjusted in response to changes in financial circumstances. Over the past decade or so, banks have become willing to consider "margin trading" when a client requires a dealing limit larger than the bank is prepared to provide. Under this arrangement, the client places a certain amount of collateral with the bank and can then trade much larger amounts. This practice often is used with leveraged and hedge funds. Also, most institutions place separate limits on the value of contracts that mature in a single day with a single customer, and some restrict dealings with certain customers to spot only, unless there are compensating balances. A bank's procedures for evaluating credit risk and controlling exposure are reviewed by bank supervisory authorities as part of the regular examination process.

◗ Settlement Risk—A Form of Credit Risk

It was noted in Chapter 2 that foreign exchange trading is subject to a particular form of credit risk known as settlement risk or Herstatt risk, which stems in part from the fact that the two legs of a foreign exchange transaction are often settled in two different time zones, with different business hours. Also noted was the fact that market participants and central banks have undertaken considerable initiatives in recent years to reduce Herstatt risk. Two such efforts are worth mentioning.

In October 1994, the New York Foreign Exchange Committee, a private-sector group sponsored by the Federal Reserve Bank of New York, published a study entitled *Reducing Foreign Exchange Settlement Risk*, which examined the problem of settlement risk from a broad perspective. The Committee found that foreign exchange settlement risk is much greater than previously recognized and lasts longer than just the time zone differences in different markets. In the worst case, a firm can

be "at risk" for as long as 72 hours between the time it issues an irrevocable payment instruction on one leg of the transaction and the time payment is received irrevocably and unconditionally on the other leg. The Committee recommended a series of private sector "best practices" to help reduce Herstatt risk, including establishing arrangements to net payments obligations, setting prudent exposure limits, and reducing the time taken for reconciliation procedures.

More recently, in March 1996, the central banks of the major industrial nations issued a report through the Bank for International Settlements, called *Settlement Risk in Foreign Exchange Transactions*, which highlighted the pervasive dimensions of settlement risk, expressed concern about the problem, and suggested an approach for dealing with it. The report confirmed the finding of the New York Foreign Exchange Committee that foreign exchange settlement exposure can last up to several days, and it recommended a three-track strategy calling for:

◗ individual banks to improve management and control of their foreign exchange settlement exposures;

◗ industry groups in the private sector to provide services that will contribute to the risk reduction efforts of individual banks; and

◗ central banks to improve national payment systems and otherwise stimulate appropriate private sector actions.

Some steps have been taken to reduce settlement risk, and others are being considered to help deal with this problem. There are "back-end" solutions, using netting and exchange clearing arrangements to modify the settlement process,

BOX 8-1

ARRANGEMENTS FOR DEALING WITH SETTLEMENT RISK

One of the aims of netting is to reduce settlement risk by providing for an agreed offsetting of positions or obligations by trading partners. Netting can take either a *bilateral* or a *multilateral* form. *Bilateral* netting is designed to reduce counterparty exposure by automatically offsetting concurrent obligations of each of two parties to the other. *Multilateral* netting extends this practice to more than two participants—calculating each participant's "net-net" position, or position against the group of participants as a whole and settling through a central party. In recent years, a number of procedural and legal changes have been introduced in various countries to facilitate netting arrangements.

Bilateral netting arrangements for foreign exchange were introduced a number of years ago, through facilities in FXNET, SWIFT, and VALUENET.

More comprehensive, *multilateral* netting schemes were subsequently introduced, operating through *ECHO* (or exchange clearing house) and *Multinet*. The two competing systems subsequently merged.

Some of the new "front-end" approaches—all of which are in various stages of study and development—reflect the fact that *cash delivery* of the various currencies is needed by the participants in only a small percentage of foreign exchange transactions.

One novel "front-end" approach designed to reduce settlement risk from foreign exchange trades beyond conventional bilateral netting systems is called "netting +." Under this technique, each day (say, day 1) two "netting +" counterparties scheduled to settle a dollar amount for a non-dollar amount "tomorrow" (day 2) will, instead, arrange a "tom-next" (or tomorrow/next day) swap for the non-dollar amount and the dollar equivalent, effectively rolling forward the settlement one day (to day 3) and combining it with other settlements scheduled for that day. The only payment (on day 2) is a (usually relatively small) dollar amount to cover any difference between the contracted price and that day's market price.[5] This approach is in the developmental stage.

Another experimental "front-end" approach is "foreign exchange difference settled" (FXDS), under which the two counterparties, instead of exchanging two full payments at settlement, agree to settle only the net amount by which the relevant values of the two currencies have changed.

A group of leading international institutions called the "Group of 20" has proposed a concept of "continuous linked settlement" (CLS) for reducing settlement risk, in which a specialized bank would act as clearing institution, providing for "real time" settlement—payment versus payment, or "PVP," in major currencies among participating institutions. The participants expect the system to begin operating in the year 2000.

and "front-end" solutions, which change the nature of the trade at the outset, modifying what is to be exchanged at settlement. (See Box 8-1.)

Steps have also been taken to improve central bank services in order to reduce foreign exchange settlement risk. At the beginning of 1998, the Federal Reserve extended Fedwire operating hours. Fedwire is now open 18 hours a day. Its operational hours overlap with the national payment systems in all other major financial centers around the world. Similarly, CHIPS has expanded its hours and introduced other improvements.

▶ **Sovereign Risk—A Form of Credit Risk**
Another element of credit risk of importance in foreign exchange trading is *sovereign risk*—that is, the political, legal, and other risks associated with a cross-border payment. At one time or another, many governments have interfered with international transactions in their currencies. Although in today's liberalized markets and less regulated environment there are fewer and fewer restrictions imposed on international payments, the possibility that a country may prohibit a transfer cannot be ignored—the United States Government has imposed such restrictions on various occasions. In order to limit their exposure to this risk, banks and other foreign exchange market participants sometimes establish ceilings for individual countries, monitor regulatory changes, watch credit ratings, and, where practicable, obtain

export risk guaranties and other forms of insurance.

▶ **Group of Thirty Views on Credit Risk**
As with market risk, the management of credit risk has become more complicated and more sophisticated with the development of derivative instruments and, more generally, the evolution of financial markets. The Group of Thirty report, *Derivatives: Practices and Principles*, addressed questions of measuring, monitoring, and managing credit risk in derivatives activity. The report recommended that each dealer and end-user of derivatives should assess the credit risk arising from derivatives activities based on frequent measures of current and potential exposure against credit limits. It further recommended that dealers and end-users use one master agreement as widely as possible, and that each counterparty document existing and future derivatives transactions, including foreign exchange forwards and options, and cover various types of "netting" arrangements. The report also recommended that regulators and supervisors recognize the benefits of netting arrangements and encourage their wider use.

More recently, other ideas have been put forward for a portfolio approach to credit risk, similar to the value-at-risk approach to market risk. The aim would be to produce a single number for how much a bank stands to lose on a portfolio of credits of varying characteristics, and thus to determine how much the bank should hold in reserve against that portfolio.

---

3. Other Risks

Numerous other forms of risk can be involved in foreign exchange trading, just as in other financial activities.

Trading activities are subject to *liquidity risk*, since in times of stress market liquidity can change significantly and rapidly—within the course of a day, or, in extreme cases, within minutes—and a bank may find itself unable to liquidate assets quickly without loss or to manage unplanned decreases or changes in funding sources. Given the size, breadth, and depth of the foreign exchange market, liquidity risk is less a danger than in most financial markets.

There are *legal risks*, or the risk of loss that a contract cannot be enforced, which may occur, for example, because the counter-party is not legally capable of making the binding agreement, or because of insufficient documentation or a contract in conflict with statutes or regulatory policy. While such legal risks are encountered in traditional banking, they have taken new forms with the growth in derivatives, since many existing laws and regulations were written before these products and transactions came into

being, and it is not clear how the laws and regulations apply.

Also, foreign exchange trading and other financial businesses face considerable *operational risks*—that is, the risk of losses from inadequate systems, human error, or a lack of proper oversight policies and procedures and management control. There are numerous examples of problems and failures in financial institutions around the world related to inadequate systems and controls—although employee dishonesty of one sort or another is very often involved.

All of these risks develop, evolve, and mutate as conditions change and new foreign exchange techniques and instruments are created. In foreign exchange trading, as in other banking and financial transactions, the matter of managing risk is a continuous and exacting part of doing business.

CHAPTER 9

During the first decade and a half after World War II, the United States monetary authorities did not actively intervene or directly operate in the foreign exchange market for the purpose of influencing the dollar exchange rate or exchange market conditions Under the Bretton Woods par value exchange rate system, the obligation of the United States was to assure the gold convertibility of the dollar at $35 per ounce to the central banks and monetary authorities of IMF members. The actions of other governments, intervening in dollars as appropriate to keep their own currencies within the one percent of dollar par value that IMF rules required, maintained the day-to-day market level of the dollar within those narrow margins Under that arrangement, the United States played only a passive role in the determination of exchange rates in the market: In a system of "n" currencies, not every one of the "n" countries can independently set its own exchange rate against the others Such a system would be over-determined At least one currency must be passive, and the dollar served as that "nth" currency

In the early 1960s, the United States became more active in exchange market operations. By then, the United States had begun to experience its own serious and prolonged balance of payments problems. Increasingly, the United States became concerned about protecting its gold stock and maintaining the credibility of the dollar's link to gold and the official gold price of $35 per ounce on which the world par value system of exchange rates was based.

The Bretton Woods fixed exchange rate system became unsustainable over time—it broke down in 1971 and finally collapsed in 1973. In 1978, after much of the world had moved *de facto* to a floating exchange rate system, the IMF Articles were amended to change the basic obligation of IMF members. No longer were members obliged to maintain par values; instead, they were "to collaborate with the Fund and other members to assure orderly exchange arrangements and to promote a stable system of exchange rates." Each member was authorized to adopt the exchange arrangement of its choice—fixed or floating, tied to another currency or to a basket of currencies—subject, in all cases, to general obligations of the IMF: to avoid exchange rate manipulation; to promote orderly economic, financial, and monetary conditions; and to foster orderly economic growth with reasonable price stability. U.S. law was amended to authorize the United States to accept the obligations introduced in the 1978 IMF amendment.

Today, the basic exchange rate obligation of IMF members continues as set forth in the 1978 amendment. Under provisions of that amendment, each member is required to notify the Fund of the exchange arrangements it will

apply in fulfillment of its IMF obligations.

Currently, the exchange rate regime of the United States is recorded by the IMF under the classification of "Independent Floating," with the notation that the exchange rate of the dollar is determined freely in the foreign exchange market. Of course, the United States does on occasion intervene in the foreign exchange market, as described below. However, in recent periods such occasions have been rare; the United States has intervened only when there was a clear and convincing case that intervention was called for.

---

1. U.S. Foreign Exchange Operations Under Bretton Woods

During the Bretton Woods years, although there were a number of changes in various nations' par values, exchange rate fluctuations were relatively modest most of the time. However, exchange market pressures showed in other ways. Much attention was paid to the size of U.S. gold reserves in relation to the size of U.S. official dollar liabilities—the dollar balances held by official institutions in other countries. Various measures were taken to protect the U.S. gold stock and the credibility of dollar convertibility for foreign official holders. Many actions were taken by the U.S. authorities to hold down the growth of what foreign central banks might regard as their "excess" dollar balances, with a view to reducing the pressure for conversion of official dollar holdings into gold. Specific U.S. actions taken during the Bretton Woods par value period included:

▶ borrowing foreign currencies from foreign monetary authorities through reciprocal credit lines (swap lines) for the purpose of selectively buying dollars from certain foreign

central banks that might otherwise have sought to convert those dollars into gold;

▶ selling foreign-currency-denominated bonds (called Roosa bonds after the then Under-Secretary of the Treasury) to mop up excess dollars that might otherwise be converted by foreign central banks into gold;

▶ acquiring foreign currencies by drawing down the U.S. reserve position at the IMF, again using those currencies to buy excess dollars from other central banks and also to pay off swap debts;

▶ cooperating with monetary authorities of other major countries to buy and sell gold in the free market to maintain the *free market* dollar price of gold close to the *official* price of $35 per ounce; and

▶ intervening, on occasion, *directly* in the foreign exchange market during the 1960s and early 1970s in order to reduce the pressures to convert dollars into gold, and to maintain or restore orderly conditions in volatile currency markets.

BOX 9-1

AUTHORIZATION AND MANAGEMENT OF INTERVENTION OPERATIONS

By law and custom, the Secretary of the Treasury is primarily and directly responsible to the President and the Congress for formulating and defending U.S. domestic and international economic policy, assessing the position of the United States in the world economy, and conducting international negotiations on these matters. At the same time, foreign exchange markets are closely linked to money markets and to questions of monetary policy that are within the purview of the Federal Reserve. There is a distinct role and responsibility for the Federal Reserve, working with the Treasury and in cooperation with foreign central banks that operate in their own markets. For many years, the Treasury and the Federal Reserve have recognized the need to cooperate in the formulation and implementation of exchange rate policy.

The Treasury and the Federal Reserve each have independent legal authority to intervene in the foreign exchange market. Since 1978, the financing of U.S. exchange market operations has generally been shared between the two. Intervention by the Treasury is authorized by the Gold Reserve Act of 1934 and the Bretton Woods Agreements Act of 1944. Intervention by the Federal Reserve System is authorized by the Federal Reserve Act. It is clear that the Treasury cannot commit Federal Reserve funds to intervention operations. It also is clear that any foreign exchange operations of the Federal Reserve will be conducted, in the words of the Federal Open Market Committee (FOMC), "in close and continuous cooperation with the United States Treasury." In practice, any differences between the Treasury and the Federal Reserve on these matters have generally been worked out satisfactorily. Cooperation is facilitated by the fact that all U.S. foreign exchange market operations are conducted by the Foreign Exchange Desk of the Federal Reserve Bank of New York, acting as agent for both the Treasury and the Federal Reserve System.

The Treasury's foreign exchange operations are financed through the Exchange Stabilization Fund (ESF) of the Treasury. The ESF was created in the early 1930s, utilizing profits resulting from the increase in the official dollar price of gold enacted at that time. The ESF is available to the Secretary of the Treasury, with the approval of the President, for trading in gold and foreign exchange.

The Federal Reserve's foreign exchange operations are financed through a System account in which all 12 Federal Reserve Banks participate. The System account operates under the guidance of the FOMC, the System's principal policy-making body. Transactions are executed by the Federal Reserve Bank of New York, under the direction of the Manager of the System Open Market Account, who is responsible for operations of both the Domestic Desk and the Foreign Exchange Desk.

Three formal documents of the FOMC provide direction and oversight for the System's foreign exchange operations and set forth guidance for the Federal Reserve Bank of New York in conducting these operations. The three documents, which are subject to annual FOMC approval and amended as appropriate, are (1) the *Authorization* for Foreign Currency Operations, (2) the Foreign Currency *Directive*, and (3) the *Procedural Instructions*. They provide the framework within which the Foreign Exchange Desk of the Federal Reserve Bank of New York conducts foreign exchange operations for the

(continued on page 88)

(continued from page 87)

System. The aim is to assure FOMC guidance and oversight of System operations in foreign exchange while providing the Foreign Exchange Desk with the flexibility to act promptly and respond to changing market circumstances.

▶ The *Authorization* sets forth the basic structure for carrying out System foreign exchange operations, and sets limits on the size of open (or uncovered) positions in foreign currencies that can be taken in these operations.

▶ The *Directive* states that System operations in foreign currencies shall generally be directed at "countering disorderly market conditions," and provides general guidance on the transactions to be undertaken for that purpose. The Directive specifically provides that System foreign currency operations shall be conducted "in close and continuous consultation and cooperation with the United States Treasury" and "in a manner consistent with the obligations of the United States in the International Monetary Fund."

▶ The *Procedural Instructions* set forth the arrangements whereby the Foreign Exchange Desk consults and obtains clearance from the FOMC, its Foreign Currency Subcommittee, or the Federal Reserve Chairman for any operations of a certain type or magnitude between FOMC meetings. In addition to establishing the framework for Federal Reserve System foreign currency operations through these formal documents, the FOMC receives at each of its scheduled meetings a report by the Manager of the System Open Market Account of any U.S. intervention operations that have taken place since the previous meeting, and the circumstances of the operations. Formal FOMC approval is required of all operations financed through the System account.

The FOMC also is responsible for any authorization of *warehousing* foreign currencies for the Treasury and Exchange Stabilization Fund. Warehousing is a mechanism whereby the Federal Reserve can—at its sole discretion—enter into temporary swap transactions with the Exchange Stabilization Fund of the Treasury, providing dollars in exchange for an equivalent amount of foreign currency, with an agreement to reverse the payments at a specified exchange rate at a specified future date. Thus, the warehousing facility can temporarily supplement the U.S. dollar resources of the Treasury and the ESF for financing their purchases of foreign currencies and related international operations against deposits of foreign currencies. All exchange rate risk is borne by the Treasury. Warehousing transactions have been undertaken on many occasions over a long period of years.

2. U.S. Foreign Exchange Operations Since The Authorization In 1978 of Floating Exchange Rates

Since the authorization of floating in the 1978 amendment of the IMF articles, U.S. intervention operations generally have been carried out under the broad rubric of "countering disorderly market conditions." However, that general objective has been interpreted in quite different ways at different times over that period, and the approach to exchange market intervention has varied with the interpretation. During some periods, "countering disorderly market conditions" has been interpreted very narrowly, and intervention has been limited to rare and extreme situations; during other periods, it has been interpreted broadly and operations have been extensive.

During the first dozen years after exchange rate floating was sanctioned by 1978 IMF amendment, the United States changed its approach and its goals several times. There were a number of key turning points, and the U.S. experience from 1978 to 1990 breaks down into *five* distinct periods.

The first period covered the years after the amendment of the IMF articles in 1978 until early 1981. During 1978, the dollar was under heavy downward market pressure and the exchange rate declined sharply, at a time of rising international oil prices, high U.S. inflation, and a deteriorating balance of payments. In November 1978, a major new dollar support program was introduced, based on the conclusion that "the dollar's decline had gone beyond what could be justified by underlying conditions," and the U.S. authorities announced that a major effort would be undertaken to reverse the dollar's decline. The program provided for raising a large war chest of up to $30 billion equivalent in foreign currencies—by Treasury borrowing of foreign currencies in overseas capital markets, U.S. drawings from its reserve position in the IMF, sales of a portion of Treasury's gold and SDR holdings, as well as by other means. With this war chest—and supported by tighter Federal Reserve monetary policy—the United States began to intervene much more forcefully in the exchange market, often in coordinated

operations with other central banks. The decline in the dollar was halted, and after the fundamental change in Federal Reserve operating techniques and the tightening of monetary policy in October 1979, the dollar strengthened, enabling the authorities to intervene on the other side of the market during 1980 and early 1981 to recoup much of the foreign currency that had been used for earlier dollar support.

The second period covered the years from early 1981 to 1985. After the election of President Reagan, the U.S. Administration interpreted the goal of countering disorderly markets very narrowly. The authorities maintained a hands-off approach, and intervention in the exchange market was minimal. During this period, the dollar exchange rate rose strongly, in an environment of a robust U.S. economy, large budget deficits, and a tight monetary policy with interest rates that were very high by international standards.

The third period covered the time from early 1985 until February 1987. The dollar eased somewhat in the spring and summer of 1985, and an important turning point occurred at the meeting of the United States and its major industrial allies in the Group of Five—France, Germany, Japan, and the United Kingdom—at the Plaza Hotel in New York in September 1985. The dollar was still at very high levels that caused concern in the United States and abroad. In the United States there was considerable apprehension about declining U.S. competitiveness and a loss of industrial output to overseas production, and a fear of rising protectionism. Also, there was a widespread belief that the exchange rates of the major currencies against the dollar did not reflect economic fundamentals. Against this background, the finance ministers and central bank governors of the G-5 reached an agreement that an appreciation of foreign currencies relative to the dollar was desirable. In the weeks following the Plaza meeting, there were substantial intervention sales of dollars for other G-5 currencies by the United States and by other monetary authorities. U.S. intervention sales of dollars were confined to rising markets—on occasions after the dollar eased, the United States moved in to resist market pressures that would otherwise have tended to raise it back to pre-existing higher levels. The dollar declined significantly during 1985 and continued to decline during 1986, even though there was no further U.S. market intervention after the first few weeks following the Plaza agreement.

The fourth period was from February 1987 to the end of that year. By early 1987, eighteen months after the Plaza agreement, the dollar had declined to its lowest levels since 1980. With a growing trade deficit and a weakening U.S. economy, the prospect of further declines in the dollar had become a cause of concern, particularly in Europe and Japan. Six major industrial nations (the Group of Five plus Italy) met at the Louvre in Paris in February and issued a statement that their currencies were "within ranges broadly consistent with underlying economic fundamentals." They agreed "to foster stability of exchange rates around current levels." The United States, frequently in coordinated operations with other central banks, intervened on a number of occasions to buy dollars and resist the dollar's decline. But despite the intervention, the dollar continued to decline irregularly over the remainder of 1987. Many market analysts argued that the dollar's decline reflected rifts among the major G-7 nations over monetary and fiscal policies. There was concern about the risks of the situation, particularly at the time of the U.S. stock market crash in October. These uncertainties continued until the beginning of 1988, at which time, following visible, concerted, and very aggressive intervention operations by the

United States and others, the dollar stabilized and reversed its direction.

In the fifth period, covering 1988 to 1990, the dollar again trended upward, and the United States intervened, at times very heavily, in the interest of exchange rate stability, to resist upward pressure on the dollar. Once again, these operations were undertaken after statements from the Group of Seven (The Group of Five plus Italy and Canada) emphasized the importance of maintaining exchange rate stability. The G-7 issued a statement expressing concern that the continued rise of the dollar was "inconsistent with longer-run fundamentals" and that a further rise of the dollar above then-current levels, or an excessive decline, could adversely affect prospects for the world economy. The level of U.S. intervention operations during 1989 was particularly high by earlier standards, resulting in the accumulation of substantial U.S. reserve balances of foreign currencies, namely Deutsche marks and yen. This was the first time that the United States had held "owned," or non-borrowed, foreign currency reserves in large amounts.

Since 1990, the general approach has been to allow considerable scope for market forces, with intervention from time to time to resist moves that seem excessive in either direction. The U.S. authorities have on occasion sold dollars when the currency was deemed to be getting "too strong" relative to economic fundamentals and bought when it was regarded as becoming "too weak"—but the occasions have been infrequent. Operations have been modest in amounts, and often undertaken in coordinated operations with other G-7 authorities—in particular, when these other countries were concerned about the mirror image position of their own currencies, and the effect of movements in the dollar exchange rate on their own currencies. There is a recognition of the benefits and the limitations of intervention (discussed in Chapter 11), and of the situations and policy framework in which it is likely to be most helpful.

During the 1990s, there has been intervention by the U.S. authorities on both sides of the market—that is, buying dollars from time to time to resist downward pressure on the dollar exchange rate and selling dollars on a few occasions of strong upward pressure.

In 1991 and 1992, the U.S. intervened on *both* sides, buying a total of $2,659 million in dollars and selling a total of $750 million.

From 1993 through mid-1995, market pressures against the dollar were mainly downward, and the U.S. authorities intervened to buy dollars on 18 trading days, with purchases totaling $14 billion, just over half of which were purchased against yen, with the remainder purchased against marks. (For many years, the mark and the yen have been the only two currencies in which the United States has conducted its intervention operations.)

From mid-1995 until mid-1998, there were no dollar intervention operations undertaken by the U.S. authorities.

In mid-1998, the U.S. authorities re-entered the market, in cooperation with the Japanese authorities, to sell dollars for yen in an environment of weakness in the yen exchange rate.

All U.S. intervention operations in the foreign exchange market are publicly reported on a quarterly basis, a few weeks after the close of the period. These reports, entitled "Treasury and Federal Reserve Foreign Exchange Operations," are presented by the Manager of the System Open Market Account and are published by the Federal Reserve Bank of New York and in the *Federal Reserve Bulletin*. Each report documents any U.S. intervention activities of the previous quarter, describing the market environment in which they were conducted. This series provides a record of U.S. actions in the foreign exchange market for the period since 1961.

---

3. Executing Official Foreign Exchange Operations

In some countries the central bank serves as the government's principal banker, or only banker, for international payments. In such cases, the central bank may buy and sell foreign exchange, not only for foreign exchange intervention purposes, but also for such purposes as paying government bills, servicing foreign currency debts, and executing transactions for the national post office, railroads, and power company.

The Federal Reserve Bank of New York conducts all U.S. intervention operations in the foreign exchange market on behalf of the U.S.

monetary authorities. It also conducts certain non-intervention business transactions on behalf of various U.S. Government agencies. Given the vast array of international activities in which U.S. Government departments and agencies are involved, it is left to individual agencies to acquire the foreign currencies needed for their operations in the most economical way they can find. Today, only a fraction of the U.S. Government's total foreign exchange transactions are funneled through the Federal Reserve Bank of New York; the bulk of such transactions go directly through commercial or other channels.

Even so, the Foreign Exchange Desk of the Federal Reserve Bank of New York is routinely engaged in foreign exchange transactions on behalf of "customers." Thus, when operating in the foreign exchange market, the Desk is not necessarily "intervening" to influence the dollar exchange rate or conditions in the dollar market. It simply may be executing "customer" business. The customer may be another official body, and the Federal Reserve may be either helping a foreign central bank get the best available price for some commercial or financial transaction or helping that central bank (with that bank's own resources) intervene in its own currency, perhaps when its own market is closed.

There are many central bank correspondents holding dollar balances at the New York Fed, with bills to pay in non-dollar currencies, who find it convenient and economical to obtain their needed currencies through the Fed. Similarly, the New York Fed transacts customer-based foreign exchange business for a number of international institutions that hold dollar balances at the Fed.

But it is the intervention activity—circumstances, amounts, techniques, policy environment surrounding intervention operations, and possible effectiveness of such operations in influencing the exchange rate or market conditions—that is of particular interest and attracts the most attention.

▶ **Techniques of Intervention**
Techniques of intervention can differ, depending on the objective and market conditions at the time. The intervention may be coordinated with other central banks or undertaken by a single central bank operating alone. The situation may call for an aggressive action, intended to change existing attitudes about the authorities' views and intentions, or it may call for reassuring action to calm

markets. The aim may be to reverse, resist, or support a market trend. Operations may be announced or unannounced. Central banks may operate openly and directly, or through brokers and agents. They may deal with many banks or few, in sudden bursts, or slowly and steadily. They may want the operations to be visible or they may want to operate discreetly. Different objectives may require different approaches.

In the foreign exchange operations undertaken on behalf of the United States authorities, the Federal Reserve Bank of New York has, over the years, used various intervention techniques, depending on the policy objective, market conditions, and an assessment of what appears likely to be effective. In recent years, most U.S. intervention has been conducted openly, directly with a number of commercial banks and other participants in the interbank market, with the expectation that the intervention would be seen very quickly and known by the entire foreign exchange market, both in the United States and abroad. The aim has been to show a presence in the market and indicate a view about exchange rate trends. On recent occasions, there have been accompanying statements by the Secretary of the Treasury or another senior Treasury official announcing or confirming the operations.

At the New York Fed, the Foreign Exchange Desk monitors the foreign exchange market on a continuing basis, watching the market and keeping up-to-date with significant develop-ments that may be affecting the dollar and other major currencies. The Desk staff tracks market conditions around the clock during periods of stress. Federal Reserve staff, like others in the market, sit in a trading room surrounded by screens, telephones, and computers, watching the rates, reading the continuous outpouring of data, analyses, and news developments, listening over the brokers' boxes to the flow of transactions, and talking on the telephone with other market players to try to get a full understanding of different market views on what is happening and likely to happen and why. Quite importantly, the Desk personnel also stay in close touch with their counterparts in the central banks of the other major countries—both in direct one-to-one calls and through regularly scheduled conference calls—to keep informed on developments in those other markets, to hear how the other central banks assess developments and their own aims, and to discuss with them emerging trends and possible actions. The staff on the Foreign Exchange Desk of the New York Fed confers regularly, several times a day, with staff both at the Treasury and at the Federal Reserve Board of Governors in Washington, reporting the latest developments and assessments about market trends and conditions.

4. Reaching Decisions on Intervention

There is no fixed or formal procedure in the United States for reaching decisions on intervention. On occasions there may be a major agreement among the main industrial countries to follow a particular approach—for example, the decisions at the Plaza in 1985 and at the Louvre in 1987 required a coordinated approach toward the exchange market that had major implications for intervention. There may be other occasions, when the U.S. authorities conclude that some action or change in approach is needed, and they may want to discuss intervention informally with other major countries to see whether coordinated action is possible. In still other situations, when either the Treasury or the Federal Reserve believes a change in approach is called for, there will be discussions among senior U.S. officials of that viewpoint. Indeed, there are any number of possible way in which questions of exchange rate policy can by considered.

When the Desk does undertake intervention purchases or sales, the financing is usually split evenly between the Treasury's Exchange Stabilization Fund and the Fed's System Open Market Account. However, there are occasions when, for technical or other reasons, the financing for a particular operation is booked entirely by the Treasury or the Federal Reserve.

The dollar amount of any U.S. foreign exchange market intervention is routinely sterilized—that is, the effect on the monetary base, plus or minus, is promptly offset. Indeed, it is generally the practice in most major industrial countries to sterilize intervention operations, at least over a period of time. Thus, any expansion (or contraction) in the monetary base resulting from selling (or buying) dollars in the foreign exchange market would be automatically offset by the Federal Reserve's domestic monetary actions. While the sterilized foreign exchange market intervention does not itself affect the U.S. money stock, that does not imply that conditions in the foreign exchange market do not influence monetary policy decisions—at times they clearly do. But that influence shows up as a deliberate monetary policy decision, rather than as a side effect of the foreign exchange market intervention.

5. Financing Foreign Exchange Intervention

All foreign exchange operations by the monetary authorities must, of course, be financed. In the case of a foreign central bank operating in dollars to influence the exchange rate for its currency, that simply may mean transfers into or out of its dollar accounts (held at the Federal Reserve Bank of New York or at commercial banks) as it buys and sells dollars in the market. For the United States, it currently means adding to or reducing the foreign currency balances held by the Treasury and the Federal Reserve. However, U.S. techniques for acquiring resources for exchange market operations have gone through several phases.

During the late 1940s and the 1950s, under the Bretton Woods system, the United States kept its reserves almost entirely in the form of *gold*, and did not hold significant foreign currency balances. Since the U.S. role in the foreign exchange markets was entirely passive, market intervention and financing market intervention were not an issue.

In the early 1960s, when the United States began to operate more actively in the foreign exchange market and was reluctant to draw down its gold stock, the U.S. authorities began the practice of establishing *reciprocal currency arrangements*—or *swap* lines—with central banks and other monetary authorities abroad, as a means of gaining rapid access to foreign currencies for market intervention and other purposes.

These reciprocal swap lines were developed as a technique for prearranging short-term credits among central banks and treasuries, enabling them to borrow each other's currencies—if both sides agreed—at a moment's notice, in event of need. Over time, a network of these facilities was built up, mainly between the Federal Reserve and the major foreign central banks and the Bank for International Settlements (BIS), although the Treasury also has swap lines. These facilities have enabled the United States to acquire foreign currencies when they were needed for foreign exchange operations, and from time to time some of the swap partners drew on the facilities to obtain dollars they needed for their own market operations.

An advantage of the central bank reciprocal swap lines was that drawings could be activated quickly and easily, in case of mutual consent. A drawing could be initiated by a phone call followed by an exchange of cables in which particular terms and conditions were specified within the standard framework of the swap agreement. Technically, a central bank swap drawing consists of a spot transaction and a forward exchange transaction in the opposite direction. Thus, the Federal Reserve might sell spot dollars for, say marks, to the German central bank, and simultaneously contract to buy back the same amount of dollars three months later. By mutual agreement, the drawing might be rolled over for additional three-month periods.

Central bank swap lines were used actively by the United States in periods of exchange market pressure during the 1960s and 1970s, when the United States did not hold substantial foreign currency balances. They had important advantages, but also some limitations. To be activated, swap drawings required the consent of both parties. They did not provide foreign currencies to the borrower unless the partner central bank agreed. As with any credit, availability can be made subject to policy or other conditions imposed by the creditor that the borrower might not like. Also, swap drawings were technically short term, requiring agreement every three months for a rollover.

In November 1978, when the U.S. authorities wanted to correct what was regarded as an excessive decline in the dollar's value in the exchange market, they decided to increase by a substantial amount their "*owned reserves*," or foreign currency balances fully available to them and under their own control, and not be restricted to "borrowed reserves," or balances available from, and limited by, swap arrangements. The U.S. authorities wanted to show their determination to support and strengthen the dollar by taking new, innovative, and unprecedented actions, and by building up a large supply of foreign currencies that could be used by the United States at its sole discretion for aggressive intervention.

Accordingly, to increase its "owned reserves," the United States Treasury announced that it would draw $3 billion worth of marks and yen from the U.S. reserve position in the IMF; that it would sell $2 billion equivalent of IMF Special Drawing Rights (SDR) for marks, yen, and Swiss francs; and, as a major innovation, that it would, for the first time, *borrow foreign currencies in overseas markets*. The U.S. Treasury was prepared to issue foreign currency-denominated securities up to the equivalent of $10 billion.

Between November 1978 and January 1981, foreign currency-denominated securities (called Carter bonds) were issued amounting to the equivalent of approximately $6.5 billion, all in German marks and Swiss francs. All of these securities were redeemed by mid-1983. The dollar strengthened during the period when the securities were outstanding, and the Treasury made a profit on the amounts of borrowed currencies that were used for intervention when the dollar was low and bought back when the dollar was higher. In the early 1980s, the United States was able to move to a modest net positive foreign currency position, with foreign currency balances somewhat in excess of its foreign currency liabilities.

The next important change in this situation occurred in the late 1980s, when the U.S. authorities *built up their foreign currency balances* to far higher levels than ever before. During periods of strong upward pressure on the dollar exchange rate, the United States intervened in substantial amounts to resist what was regarded as excessive upward pressure on the dollar, and acquired substantial balances of marks and yen. As of the middle of 1988, the United States held foreign currency balances of only *$10 billion*. But by the end of 1990, the United States reported foreign currency balances of more than *$50 billion*. Since then, there has been some net use of these balances for intervention purposes, and some reduction through exchanges of U.S. foreign currency balances for dollars with the issuers of those currencies, when both parties felt they were holding excess amounts relative to their needs. In June 1998, the U.S. authorities held $30 billion in marks and yen; these balances are marked-to-market on a monthly basis. U.S. holdings of international reserves (excluding gold), measured relative to imports or size of the economy, still remain well below the levels of many other major industrial nations.

The reciprocal currency arrangements, or swap lines, remain in place, and are available if needed. At present, the Federal Reserve has such arrangements with 14 foreign central banks and the Bank for International Settlements, totaling $32.4 billion (Figure 9-1). For many years, however, the United States has not drawn on any of the swap lines for financing U.S. intervention or for any other purpose. There have been drawings on both Federal Reserve and Treasury ESF swap facilities initiated by the other party to the swap—in particular, swap lines have

--------- **FIGURE 9-1**

FEDERAL RESERVE RECIPROCAL CURRENCY ARRANGEMENTS (MILLIONS OF DOLLARS)

Institution	Amount of Facility	Outstanding as of December 31, 1997
Austrian National Bank	250	0
National Bank of Belgium	1,000	0
Bank of Canada	2,000	0
National Bank of Denmark	250	0
Bank of England	3,000	0
Bank of France	2,000	0
Deutsche Bundesbank	6,000	0
Bank of Italy	3,000	0
Bank of Japan	5,000	0
Bank of Mexico	3,000	0
Netherlands Bank	500	0
Bank of Norway	250	0
Bank of Sweden	300	0
Swiss National Bank	4,000	0
Bank for International Settlements Dollars against Swiss Francs	600	0
Dollars against other Authorized European currencies	1,250	0

provided temporary financing in dealing with the Mexican financial crisis and certain earlier Latin American debt problems.

The foreign currency balances owned by the Treasury's Exchange Stabilization Fund and by the Federal Reserve System are regularly invested in a variety of instruments that have a high degree of liquidity, good credit quality, and market-related rates of return. A significant portion of the balances consists of German and Japanese government securities, held either directly or under repurchase agreement. As of June 1998, outright holdings of foreign government securities ' by U.S. monetary authorities totaled $7.1 billion, and government securities held under repurchase agreements by U.S. monetary authorities totaled $10.9 billion. The Federal Reserve Bank of New York makes these various investments for both the Treasury and the Federal Reserve, and the Desk stays in close contact with German and Japanese money market and capital market sources in arranging these transactions.

CHAPTER 10

The international monetary system is the legal and institutional framework—the laws,

rules, customs, instruments, and organizations—within which the foreign exchange

market operates Over the past 120 years, the international monetary system has gone

through major changes as it has evolved to its present structure

Some form of trading in national currencies has existed for as long as there have been national currencies and an opportunity for buyers and sellers to trade them. From antiquity, gold was used as a monetary metal, and silver—a lighter and more prevalent metal—had an equal and, for much of the time, greater monetary role. Gradually, over several decades during the nineteenth century, at a time when the role of central banks was expanding in some industrial countries and classical economics was becoming more widely accepted, the gold standard was adopted by a substantial number of nations. Not all experience with bi-mentalism had been successful, and with the discovery of extensive gold deposits in the nineteenth century, it became more feasible to have monetary systems based on gold alone.

Only when that happened was there a distinct, functioning international monetary system in the sense that we now use that term—with a set of practices and "rules of the game," accepted by a widespread membership including a large number of major nations. Specie transfers among participating countries were possible, and as more and more nations adopted the gold standard and confidence in the new system increased, it became the practice to settle many payments by debiting or crediting foreign accounts rather than by actual specie transfer. With the telegraph and, later, the telephone and other innovations, it was technologically possible to trade foreign exchange on an international basis.

Since the adoption of a system based on the gold standard around 1880, the international monetary system has gone through several distinct turning points and transformations. The history of those 120 years can be divided into four distinct periods.

1. The Gold Standard, 1880 - 1914

Britain adopted a gold standard after the Napoleonic wars in the early part of the nineteenth century. In the second half of that century, a number of nations in Europe and elsewhere followed suit, though some for a time based their currencies on a bimetallic gold/silver standard. The United States adopted the gold standard *de* *facto* in 1879, by making the "greenbacks" that the Government had issued during the Civil War period convertible into gold; it then formally adopted the gold standard by legislation in 1900. By 1914, the gold standard had been accepted by a large number of countries, although it was certainly not universal.

The "gold specie" standard called for fixed exchange rates, with parities set for participating currencies in terms of gold, and provided that any paper currency could on demand be exchanged for gold specie at the central bank of issue. The system was designed to bring automatic adjustment in case of external deficits or surpluses in transactions between countries, that is, balance of payments imbalances. The underlying concept was that any deficit country would have to surrender gold to cover its deficit, with the result that the volume of its money would be reduced, leading to lower prices, while the influx of that gold into the surplus country would expand the volume of that country's money and lead to higher prices.

In the foreign exchange market, under the gold standard, exchange rates could, in principle, fluctuate only within very narrow limits determined by the costs of shipping and insuring gold. Thus, if U.S. residents accumulated pounds sterling as a result of exporting more goods and services to Britain than they imported and being paid in pounds for the excess, the U.S. holders of sterling had the option of converting pounds into gold at par value at the Bank of England and shipping the gold back to New York. During the 1880-1914 period, the "mint parity" between the U.S. dollar and sterling was approximately $4.87, based on a U.S. official gold price of $20.67 per ounce and a U.K. official gold price of £ 4.24 per ounce. The sterling/dollar exchange rate would not fluctuate beyond the "gold points"—about three cents above and below the mint parity—which represented the cost of shipping and insuring gold, since at any exchange rate outside the gold points it would be possible to gain an arbitrage profit by converting currency into gold and shipping the gold to the other center.

While some gold transfers actually took place under this system, such shipments frequently were obviated by monetary policy moves. In the example above, the U.K. might raise interest rates to attract capital inflows—i.e., increase the demand for sterling—and counterbalance the financial impact of the import excess. Presumably, higher interest rates also would have a deflationary effect in the deficit country.

This automatic operation of the balance of payments adjustment process under the gold standard required, in theory, that in their financial policies, participating countries give an absolute priority to external adjustment over domestic objectives. This meant that in any periods of conflict between domestic and external objectives, policy tools might not be available to be used for domestic problems of recession, unemployment, or inflation. But the philosophy widely held in those pre-Keynesian times was that economies would tend naturally toward reasonably high levels of employment and reasonable price stability without such government policy actions.

Assessments still vary concerning the historical record of the period of the gold standard during its heyday. It is true that for a forty-year period there were no changes in the exchange rates of the United States, Great Britain, Germany, and France (though the same did not hold for a number of other countries). There were few barriers to gold shipments and few capital controls in the major countries. Capital flows generally seem to have played a stabilizing, rather than destabilizing, role. Advocates of the gold standard point to the benefits of stable and predictable exchange rates, and the limits the gold standard placed on the extent to which central banks could pursue inflationary monetary policies. These advocates look back with nostalgia to what they regard as a stable period of prompt and smooth external adjustment without governmental interference.

But others argue that there is more myth than reality to that view. They object to a system that they feel always subordinated domestic objectives and living standards to the requirements of international adjustment. They express concern about the rigidities of a system that tied international reserves to a commodity such as gold, whose supply depended on the limitations and uncertainties of new production and competing demands for jewelry, industrial needs, and private hoarding. They contend that things did not, in fact, work so smoothly as alleged—that governments did not always follow the "rules of the game," for example, in adjusting domestic money supply to gold reserves; that macroeconomic performance under the gold standard was not exceptional, as there were periods of inflation, deflation, and high unemployment; and that there were periodic financial crises. Their view

is that the successes associated with the gold standard resulted from special conditions of the time—a long period of political stability and economic expansion worldwide—with sterling the only international currency and London the unrivaled financial center, and with the British Commonwealth a large and rapidly growing producer of gold as important new sources were discovered.

The debate over the gold standard has continued. In 1981, President Ronald Reagan set up a U.S. Gold Commission to study a possible return to a gold standard. The Commission agreed that there is a strong need for monetary discipline but did not recommend a return to gold. At present, the opponents of a gold standard have the upper hand, and a restoration of a gold standard looks extremely unlikely in the foreseeable future.

2. The Inter - War Period, 1919 - 1939

After the outbreak of the First World War, one combatant country after another suspended gold convertibility, and floating exchange rates prevailed. The United States, which entered the war late, maintained gold convertibility, but the dollar effectively floated against the other currencies, which were no longer convertible into dollars.

After the war, and in the early and mid-twenties, many exchange rates fluctuated sharply. Most currencies experienced substantial devaluations against the dollar; the U.S. currency had greatly improved its competitive strength over European currencies during the war, in line with the strengthening of the relative position of the U.S. economy.

In Europe, especially in Great Britain, there was a widespread desire to return to the stability of the gold standard, and a worry about the growing attractiveness of the dollar—which was convertible into gold—and of dollar-denominated assets. After a lengthy internal debate, the United Kingdom reestablished gold convertibility at the pre-war parity against the U.S. dollar. The argument for restoring the pound's pre-war parity rather than a devalued rate was that the pound had to be able "to look the dollar in the eye" in order to maintain worldwide confidence in sterling and in British financial institutions. Other nations followed Britain and went back to gold, but in many cases at devalued rates.

The distortions and disequilibria that had developed during the war were not adequately reflected in the par values that were established in the mid-twenties. Notably, the pound sterling was well over-valued, leading to severe payments deficits and deflation, while the French franc was fixed at a greatly depreciated level, resulting in large balance of payments surpluses. Under heavy financial pressures, the United Kingdom abandoned the gold standard in 1931, and others followed over the next few years.

During the 1930s, exchange markets often were turbulent and disorderly. In an environment of severe global depression and a lack of confidence, the international monetary system disintegrated into rival currency blocs,

competitive devaluations, discriminatory trade restrictions and exchange controls, high tariffs, and barter trade arrangements. Against the background of widespread international monetary disorder bordering on chaos, there were several failed efforts to reestablish order.

The collapse of international trade and finance left a profound impression on those who lived through it and on subsequent generations. Unlike the heyday of the gold standard, there was never any nostalgia for a return of the financial conditions of the 1930s. Quite the contrary, it was the experience of conflict, rivalry, and nationalism in the 1930s that created much of the support for international monetary cooperation after the Second World War.

---

3. The Bretton Woods Par Value Period, 1946 - 1971

Work on plans for a postwar international monetary system started in the early years of World War II, in both the United States and United Kingdom. (Germany also broadcast reports of the kind of monetary system it was planning for the post-war world.)

There was a widespread feeling in the United Kingdom and the United States that inadequate international monetary arrangements had contributed to the Great Depression and the war, and there was a strong determination to prevent a recurrence in the future. Drafts were exchanged for several years, leading to formal negotiations near the end of the war.

The U.S. Administration wanted to build a new international monetary system based on principles of cooperation and non-discrimination. Treasury Secretary Henry Morgenthau and

Assistant Secretary Harry Dexter White envisioned a new system that would police exchange rates, mobilize international liquidity and, more generally, provide the machinery for resolving international monetary problems in a cooperative way. Many of these ideas were shared by the U.K. authorities. In particular, both the United States and the United Kingdom wanted a system of stable exchange rates, surveillance of exchange rates, financing facilities, and related arrangements by an international body. Both wanted to avoid the competitive devaluations that had been such a problem in the 1930s.

But in view of their war-ravaged economy, their thin financial resources, and their postwar goal of full employment, U.K. negotiators wanted to set up an international monetary system that would provide substantial external financing— international credit facilities with few if any conditions—and that would place automatic disciplines for adjustment on creditor nations. The U.K. wanted to establish international liquidity arrangements under which—it seemed to the U.S. negotiators—the United States, as the only major creditor nation, would have borne much or all of the international burden of external financing and adjustment.

U.S. negotiators had no interest in making the United States a passive supplier of the world's financing needs—nor did they think the Congress would approve. The United States wanted a contributory, conditional fund for providing financing, based on conservative banking concepts. Given its dominant world position at that time, the United States prevailed in these negotiations, and the U.S. plan was accepted as the blueprint of the Bretton Woods system.

What emerged from these negotiations, in terms of foreign exchange rates and markets, was an adjustable peg exchange rate regime operating under a gold exchange standard, with currencies other than the U.S. dollar convertible into the dollar, and the dollar, in turn, convertible into gold for official holders. Member countries were to maintain "stable but adjustable" par values. But there was provision for modification of a par value, with the approval of the International Monetary Fund, in the event of "fundamental disequilibrium"—a concept that was not defined, but that conveyed the idea of large and persistent payments imbalances and reserve changes. Members were expected to maintain their exchange rates within margins of one percent on either side of par value. Members other than the United States generally were expected to meet that obligation by buying and selling dollars in the exchange markets; the United States was expected to meet its obligation by standing ready to meet requests of other monetary authorities to buy or sell gold

for dollars at $35 per ounce. Other parts of the agreement called for members, after a transitional period, to eliminate exchange restrictions on international trade and current account (but not capital account) transactions, and to make their currencies "convertible" for non-residents—in the sense that non-residents receiving those currencies in current account transactions could exchange them for U.S. dollars or other desired currencies. Importantly, the agreement also provided for borrowing facilities in the IMF for nations in temporary balance of payments difficulties.

The U.S. dollar was thus accorded a central role in the Bretton Woods system. It provided the system's link to gold, in that the United States undertook to sell (and buy) gold at $35 an ounce in transactions with the financial authorities of other member countries. With that guarantee of the dollar's convertibility into gold, it was expected that other countries would hold reserves mainly in the form of dollars and the dollar would be the world's reserve currency. The dollar, defined by its gold content, served as the numeraire, or standard measure of value, for the system.

Although the Bretton Woods agreement was negotiated in 1944 and the International Monetary Fund opened for business in 1946, the system envisaged in the IMF Articles did not become fully operational for a number of years. The financial difficulties of the early postwar years were far more severe than had been expected. The war-ravaged nations of Europe and Asia were unable to undertake their IMF obligations of eliminating discrimination and exchange restrictions on current account transactions and making their currencies freely convertible into the U.S. dollar. The IMF was put on hold, and the Marshall Plan was created to help restore the economies of Europe. The

Marshall Plan, rather than the IMF, became the framework for dealing with the financial problems of the major industrial nations in the immediate postwar period.

It was not until the end of 1958 that the major European nations had gained enough financial strength that they were willing, and felt themselves able, to accept their IMF obligations and take the step of making their currencies freely convertible for non-residents into dollars and other strong currencies. Leading up to that step, during the 1950s, as strength was restored to the European and Japanese economies, their balance of payments positions progressively improved. Conversely, the United States balance of payments position progressively weakened and moved into "official settlements" deficit—that is, the United States was in deficit in the total of its current plus long-term capital account position, and foreigners as a group were acquiring more dollars than they were spending.

Initially, the U.S. balance of payments deficits had been seen as beneficial and not a problem. The counterpart of those deficits was mainly a growth in dollar balances of the nations of Europe and elsewhere—a development that was regarded as necessary for European recovery and a welcome increase in those countries' monetary reserves. But as the decade of the 1950s passed, the world dollar shortage turned into a dollar glut. As U.S. gold reserves progressively declined, and other nations' holdings of dollar balances increased, questions arose about the ability of the United States to maintain the gold convertibility of the dollar. By late 1960—less than two years after the European nations had accepted in full the obligations of participating in the Bretton Woods par value system—the United States

was experiencing the first of many gold "crises," with other countries worrying about their "excess" dollar holdings and seeking to exchange them for gold.

As Europe and Japan recovered and greatly improved their relative economic strength and competitiveness, the basic structure of the world economy changed. Some fundamental premises of the Bretton Woods par value system began to look doubtful. The United States was no longer the overwhelmingly dominant economic power, and it no longer owned such a large share of the world's monetary gold. The United States' unique role—as issuer of the world's reserve currency, preserver of the link to gold for the entire system, and passive counterparty in the exchange markets—came under severe strain. The credibility of the U.S. obligation to convert officially held dollars into gold at $35 per ounce weakened steadily over the years, as U.S. gold reserves grew smaller and smaller while other nations' cumulative dollar holdings grew vastly larger, to a level far in excess of those U.S. gold holdings.

In part, this result reflected fundamental international changes—rapid real economic growth at different rates in different countries and a concomitant growth of trade imbalances. In part, it was also a natural consequence of the Bretton Woods system. From the late 1950s, experts had spoken about the "Triffin dilemma." The problem, as pointed out by Professor Robert Triffin, was that the founders of Bretton Woods had created an international monetary system that required, and was dependent on, U.S. payments deficits for the increases in international liquidity needed to finance the system, but those very same U.S. deficits undermined the credibility of the dollar's gold convertibility and weakened confidence in that international monetary system. An expanding world economy needed an increasing level of world reserves. Reserves consisted essentially of gold and dollars. With gold production stagnant, the only way to get an increase in international reserves was for the United States to run balance of payments deficits, resulting in mounting dollar liabilities (other countries' dollar reserve holdings) and ever larger potential demands on the limited and declining U.S. gold stock.

Initially, the Triffin dilemma was seen as a longer-term danger, which would, in time, require systemic correction. More immediate attention was focused on the shorter-term concerns about the U.S. payments deficit—what caused it, how to reduce it, and how to finance it. For much of the 1960s, improvisations and innovative changes were introduced, and, for a while, considerable progress was made. These changes included a variety of measures designed to (1) restrict U.S. capital outflows, (2) strengthen the International Monetary Fund and other institutions, (3) limit upward market price pressures on gold, and (4) deal with pressures and disorderly conditions in the exchange market. Also, in 1969, an international agreement was reached to introduce a new IMF reserve asset, Special Drawing Rights

(SDRs), which was intended to supplement the U.S. dollar and provide a mechanism for expanding international liquidity without requiring additional U.S. payments deficits or additional dollar balances—a response to the Triffin dilemma.

These events had lasting effects on the evolution of the international monetary system. But the innovations introduced in the 1960s did not correct the fundamental problems of the international monetary system or eliminate the pressures on the dollar. Over time, the dollar faced increasingly greater pressures, reflecting chronic U.S. payments deficits—in part associated with the fiscal consequences of the Vietnam War and new domestic social programs in the United States, but related also to the stronger competitive position of a restored Europe and Japan—and an international monetary structure that, in the view of most authorities, could not easily be modified to reflect the changing economic realities in the world economy. On August 15, 1971, the United States, faced with rapidly mounting demands from other nations to convert their dollars into gold, suspended gold convertibility of the dollar, and the Bretton Woods par value system effectively ceased to function.

4. The Floating Rate Period, 1971 To Present

After the United States suspended convertibility of the dollar into gold in August 1971, an effort was made, in the Smithsonian Agreement of December 1971, to reestablish a viable and stable par value structure of exchange rates. Specifically, the major industrial nations in the Group of Ten—Belgium, Canada, France, Germany, Italy, Japan, the Netherlands, Sweden, the United Kingdom, and the United States—

negotiated a multilateral realignment of exchange rates designed to eliminate the overvaluation of the dollar that had developed during the Bretton Woods par value regime, by devaluing the dollar and appreciating the par values or central rates of the currencies of certain other major industrial countries. However, the adjustment worked out in the Smithsonian negotiations represented only a modest reduction in the market value of the dollar. Measured by trade-weighted averages, the dollar exchange rate was reduced by approximately 8 percent against the currencies of the other OECD countries; this adjustment was only about half as much as technicians at the U.S. Treasury thought was needed. The dollar's par value was changed from $35 per ounce of gold to $38, a devaluation of 7.9 percent. The United States agreed to the rate adjustments arranged at the Smithsonian, but was not willing under those circumstances to restore gold convertibility.

Not many months after the December 1971 Smithsonian Agreement, exchange markets again became volatile and disorderly. It was not just the dollar that was being hit—several European currencies, too, were subject to pressures of their own. Less than fifteen months after the Smithsonian realignment, the dollar was devalued for a second time, and the par value was reduced by an additional 10 percent, from $38 to $42.22 per ounce of gold. But foreign exchange markets continued to be unstable, affecting not only the dollar but several other major currencies, and in March 1973, the Group of Ten industrial nations announced that they would allow their currencies to float.

During the period between the two U.S. dollar devaluations in 1971 and 1973, discussions began in the International Monetary Fund on possible reform of the international monetary system. These discussions quickly revealed deep divergences over what kind of system should be constructed. In Europe, there was a widely held view that the failure of Bretton Woods was due to the "exorbitant privilege" of the United States in being able to finance its external deficits by issuing its own currency—dollars—which were

then held as reserves by the rest of the world. That concern led to European proposals to severely limit or eliminate the accumulation of reserve currencies, and to require the United States to settle any external deficits with "assets," such as gold or foreign currency borrowing, rather than with dollar "liabilities."

In the United States, by contrast, the failings of the Bretton Woods par value system were attributed largely to the system's rigidity and its inadequate incentives for adjustment. There was a strongly held U.S. view that any par value system, to remain viable, needed effective inducements for "adjustment" mechanisms that would provide the necessary incentives for both deficit and surplus nations to adopt policies that would eliminate their payments imbalances. Also, the United States favored more flexibility in the exchange rate system, and argued that even in a par value based system, there should be provision for floating exchange rates to be authorized in particular situations. There had been exceptions to the par value regime even during the time of Bretton Woods—Canada, among others, had floated its currency at times—but the IMF articles did not provide for that possibility.

Beginning in 1972, these issues were heavily debated, but they remained unresolved despite various efforts at compromise. As the debate continued, the world was becoming more accustomed to operating in the floating exchange rate environment that existed de facto. Also, there was growing support for a flexible, or floating, exchange rate system in academic and some U.S. legislative circles, as well as in parts of the business community. Indeed, when the world was hit by the first major oil crisis in late 1973, many expressed the view that a system of flexible exchange rates might have some advantages for dealing with the major disruptions and enormous oil financing requirements that were emerging.

By 1976, international agreement had been reached on a change in approach. The new approach was based on the concept that good international behavior depended, not on whether a country was maintaining a fixed par value or floating its currency, or pegging to another currency or basket, but rather, on which exchange rate policies and practices the country was actually following. In other words, regardless of its exchange rate regime, a nation could be pursuing either destructive exchange rate policies or internationally responsible policies, and that should be the focus of the IMF's concern. In 1978, the IMF Articles of Agreement were amended to provide each member nation with freedom to choose an exchange rate regime that it felt best suited its needs, including individual floating and joint floating regimes such as those of the European Monetary Union—subject to the "firm surveillance" of the member's policies by the IMF. Instead of requiring a particular exchange rate regime, the amended IMF articles placed obligations on members to promote exchange stability, and to "avoid manipulating exchange rates or the international monetary system in order to prevent effective balance of payments adjustment or to gain unfair competitive advantage." The amendment took effect in 1978 and continues in force today.

Accordingly, at present, IMF member nations can choose from a variety of exchange rate regimes. As shown in Figure 4-2, nearly 40 percent of the members peg their exchange rates—either to the dollar, the French franc, another currency, or to some basket or composite currency such as the SDR. The remainder either allow their currencies to float independently, like the U.S. dollar;

maintain a cooperative joint floating arrangement, like the European Monetary Union; or operate some form of managed float or limited flexibility arrangement.

The basic structure of the exchange rate regime has remained in force since the amended IMF Articles of Agreement were adopted in 1978. Individual nations and groups of nations have used different approaches within the broader framework. In the United States, the dollar has continued to float independently throughout the period, and all of the shifts that have occurred in U.S. exchange rate policy since then have been variations on the basic theme of an independently floating regime. The exchange rate arrangements among the major European economies have gone through several modifications. Other nations have experimented with other schemes. Over the years, the trend has been toward the adoption of more flexible regimes on the part of a number of nations.

Various proposals have been put forward to modify the current structure of the international monetary system—to return to a general system of fixed rates, to move to target zones, or to introduce various other concepts. Undoubtedly there will be major changes in the international financial structure in the years ahead—with the introduction of the euro, the development of emerging markets, the evolution of transitional economies, the continuing advance of technology, and globalization. But while there may be widespread interest in finding improvements, at the present time there is no agreement on fundamental changes for the basic exchange rate system. Present efforts are focused on strengthening the system of international surveillance through the IMF, by improving the flow of financial and economic data—with greater disclosure and transparency through more accurate, more complete, and more timely data collection and reporting—as well as by making surveillance more continuous and more candid. Many changes have been introduced to improve the effectiveness of IMF surveillance. Measures also are under way to broaden the IMF's focus, to enable the fund to promote the orderly liberalization of capital movements, and to strengthen its surveillance over international capital flows. But the freedom of an IMF member to select the exchange rate regime best suited to its needs remains intact.

—— **CHAPTER 11**

In simple terms, it is the interaction of supply and demand factors for two currencies in

the market that determines the rate at which they trade But what factors influence the

many thousands of decisions made each day to buy or sell a currency? How do changes

in supply and demand conditions explain the path of an exchange rate over the course

of a day, a month, or a year?

This complex issue has been extensively studied in economic literature and widely discussed among investors, officials, academicians, traders, and others. Still, there are no definitive answers. Views on exchange rate determination differ and have changed over time. No single approach provides a satisfactory explanation of exchange rate movements, particularly short- and medium-term movements, since the advent of widespread floating in the early 1970s.

Three aspects of exchange rate determination are discussed below. First, there is a brief description of some of the broad approaches to exchange rate determination. Second, there are some comments on the problems of exchange rate forecasting in practice. Third, central bank intervention and its effects on exchange rates are discussed.

---

1. Some Approaches To Exchange Rate Determination[6]

▶ **The Purchasing Power Parity Approach**
Purchasing Power Parity (PPP) theory holds that in the long run, exchange rates will adjust to equalize the relative purchasing power of currencies. This concept follows from the *law of one price*, which holds that in competitive markets, identical goods will sell for identical prices when valued in the same currency.

The law of one price relates to an individual product. A generalization of that law is the *absolute* version of PPP, the proposition that exchange rates will equate nations' overall price *levels*. More commonly used than absolute PPP is the concept of *relative* PPP, which focuses on

changes in prices and exchange rates, rather than on absolute price levels. Relative PPP holds that there will be a *change* in exchange rates proportional to the *change* in the ratio of the two nations' price levels, assuming no changes in structural relationships. Thus, if the U.S. price level rose 10 percent and the Japanese price level rose 5 percent, the U.S. dollar would depreciate 5 percent, offsetting the higher U.S. inflation and leaving the relative purchasing power of the two currencies unchanged.

PPP is based in part on some unrealistic assumptions: that goods are identical; that all goods are tradable; that there are no transportation costs, information gaps, taxes, tariffs, or restrictions of trade; and —implicitly and importantly—that exchange rates are influenced only by relative inflation rates. But contrary to the implicit PPP assumption, exchange rates also can change for reasons other than differences in inflation rates. Real exchange rates can and do change significantly over time, because of such things as major shifts in productivity growth, advances in technology, shifts in factor supplies, changes in market structure, commodity shocks, shortages, and booms.

In addition, the relative version of PPP suffers from measurement problems: What is a good starting point, or base period? Which is the appropriate price index? How should we account for new products, or changes in tastes and technology?

PPP is intuitively plausible and a matter of common sense, and it undoubtedly has some validity—significantly different rates of inflation should certainly affect exchange rates. PPP is useful in assessing long-term exchange rate trends and can provide valuable information about long-run equilibrium. But it has not met with much success in predicting exchange rate movements over short- and medium-term horizons for widely traded currencies. In the short term, PPP seems to apply best to situations where a country is experiencing very high, or even hyperinflation, in which large and continuous price rises overwhelm other factors.

▶ **The Balance of Payments and the Internal-External Balance Approach**
PPP concentrates on one part of the balance of payments—tradable goods and services—and postulates that exchange rate changes are determined by international differences in prices, or changes in prices, of tradable items.

Other approaches have focused on the balance of payments on current account, or on the balance of payments on current account plus long-term capital, as a guide in the determination of the appropriate exchange rate. But in today's world, it is generally agreed that it is essential to look at the entire balance of payments—both current and capital account transactions—in assessing foreign exchange flows and their role in the determination of exchange rates.

John Williamson and others have developed the concept of the "fundamental equilibrium exchange rate," or FEER, envisaged as the equilibrium exchange rate that would reconcile a nation's internal and external balance. In that system, each country would commit itself to a macroeconomic strategy designed to lead, in the medium term, to "internal balance"—defined as unemployment at the natural rate and minimal inflation—and to "external balance"—defined as achieving the targeted current account balance. Each country would be committed to holding its exchange rate within a band or target zone around the FEER, or the level needed to reconcile internal and external balance during the intervening adjustment period.

The concept of FEER, as an equilibrium exchange rate to reconcile internal and external balance, is a useful one. But there are practical problems in calculating FEERs. There is no unique answer to what constitutes the FEER; depending on the particular assumptions, models, and econometric methods used, different analysts could come to quite different results. The authors recognize this difficulty, and acknowledge that some allowance should be made by way of a target band around the FEER. Williamson has suggested that FEER calculations could not realistically justify exchange rate bands narrower than plus or minus 10 percent.

ALL ABOUT...

BOX 11-1

A METHODOLOGY FOR EXCHANGE RATE ASSESSMENTS

Oversight of members' exchange rate policies is at the core of the IMF's surveillance mandate. The methodology used for assessing the appropriateness of current account positions and exchange rates for major industrial countries embodies four steps:

▶ applying a trade-equation model to calculate the underlying current account positions that would emerge at prevailing market exchange rates if all countries were producing at their potential output levels;

▶ using a separate model to estimate a normal or equilibrium level of the saving-investment balance consistent with medium-run fundamentals, including the assumption that countries were operating at potential output;

▶ calculating the amount by which the exchange rate would have to change, other things being equal, to equilibrate the underlying current account position with the medium-term saving-investment norm; and

▶ assessing whether the estimates of exchange rates consistent with medium-term fundamentals suggest that any currencies are badly misaligned.

The IMF, while generally agreeing that it is not possible to identify precise "equilibrium" values for exchange rates and that point estimates of notional equilibrium rates should generally be avoided, does use a macroeconomic balance methodology to underpin its internal IMF multilateral surveillance. This mehodology, which is used for assessing the "appropriateness" of current account positions and exchange rates for major industrial countries, is described in Box 11-1.[7]

▶ **The Monetary Approach**

The monetary approach to exchange rate determination is based on the proposition that exchange rates are established through the process of balancing the total supply of, and the total demand for, the national money in each nation. The premise is that the supply of money can be controlled by the nation's monetary authorities, and that the demand for money has a stable and predictable linkage to a few key variables, including an inverse relationship to the interest rate—that is, the higher the interest rate, the smaller the demand for money.

In its simplest form, the monetary approach assumes that: prices and wages are completely flexible in both the short and long run, so that PPP holds continuously, that capital is fully mobile across national borders, and that domestic and foreign assets are perfect substitutes. Starting from equilibrium in the money and foreign exchange markets, if the U.S. money supply increased, say, 20 percent, while the Japanese money supply remained stable, the U.S. price level, in time, would rise 20 percent and the dollar would depreciate 20 percent in terms of the yen.

In this simplified version, the monetary approach combines the PPP theory with the quantity theory of money—increases or decreases in the money supply lead to proportionate increases or decreases in the price level over time, without any permanent effects on output or interest rates. More sophisticated versions relax some of the restrictive assumptions—for example, price flexibility and PPP may be assumed not to hold in the short run—but maintain the focus on the role of national monetary policies.

Empirical tests of the monetary approach—simple or sophisticated—have failed to provide an adequate explanation of exchange rate movements during the floating rate period. The approach offers only a partial view of the forces influencing exchange rates—it assumes away the role of non-monetary assets such as bonds, and it takes no explicit account of supply and demand conditions in goods and services markets.

Despite its limitations, the monetary approach offers very useful insights. It highlights the importance of monetary policy in influencing exchange rates, and correctly warns that excessive monetary expansion leads to currency depreciation.

The monetary approach also provides a basis for explaining exchange rate overshooting—a situation often observed in exchange markets in which a policy move can lead to an initial exchange rate move that exceeds the eventual change implied by the new long-term situation. In the context of monetary approach models that incorporate short-term stickiness in prices, exchange rate overshooting can occur because prices of financial assets—interest and exchange rates—respond more quickly to policy moves than does the price level of goods and services. Thus, for example, a money supply increase (or

decrease) in the United States can lead to a greater temporary dollar depreciation (appreciation) as domestic interest rates decline (rise) temporarily before the adjustment of the price level to the new long-run equilibrium is completed and interest rates return to their original levels.

▶ **The Portfolio Balance Approach**

The portfolio balance approach takes a shorter-term view of exchange rates and broadens the focus from the demand and supply conditions for money to take account of the demand and supply conditions for other financial assets as well. Unlike the monetary approach, the portfolio balance approach assumes that domestic and foreign bonds are not perfect substitutes. According to the portfolio balance theory in its simplest form, firms and individuals balance their portfolios among domestic money, domestic bonds, and foreign currency bonds, and they modify their portfolios as conditions change. It is the process of equilibrating the total demand for, and supply of, financial assets in each country that determines the exchange rate.

Each individual and firm chooses a portfolio to suit its needs, based on a variety of considerations—the holder's wealth and tastes, the level of domestic and foreign interest rates, expectations of future inflation, interest rates, and so on. Any significant change in the underlying factors will cause the holder to adjust his portfolio and seek a new equilibrium. These actions to balance portfolios will influence exchange rates.

Accordingly, a nation with a sudden increase in money supply would immediately purchase both domestic and foreign bonds, resulting in a decline in both countries' interest rates, and, to the extent of the shift to foreign bonds, a depreciation in the nation's home currency. Over time, the depreciation in the home currency would lead to growth in the nation's exports and a decline in its imports, and thus, to an improved trade balance and reversal of part of the original depreciation.

As yet, there is no unified theory of exchange rate determination based on the portfolio balance approach that has proved reliable in forecasting. In fact, results of empirical tests of the portfolio balance approach do not compare favorably with those from simpler models. These results reflect both conceptual problems and the lack of adequate data on the size and currency composition of private sector portfolios.

BOX 11-2

MEASURING THE DOLLAR'S EQUILIBRIUM VALUE:

❯ A Look at Some Alternatives

As the discussion above indicates, there are various ways of estimating the dollar's "equilibrium" value, and they can yield a wide range of possible results.

In its 1998 annual report, the Bank for International Settlements (BIS) looks at three calculations of the dollar's long-run equilibrium rate, which can be compared with the dollar's market rates.

The three calculated rates considered by the BIS are (1) Purchasing Power Parity (PPP), (2) PPP adjusted for productivity, and (3) Fundamental Equilibrium Exchange Rates (FEER).[8]

As of mid-May 1998, on the basis of a straight calculation of PPP, the dollar appeared to be undervalued in the market (see table below). On May 11, 1998 the dollar was trading at 1.77 DEM and 132 yen. But to reach parity in PPP terms, the dollar would have had to command about 15 percent more DEM and about 30 percent more yen, using end-1996 measures of PPP.

The calculations for PPP adjusted for productivity show a different picture. Some analysts contend that differences in productivity across countries distort international comparisons of broad consumption baskets used in PPP calculations. The argument is made that countries such as Japan with higher productivity in the traded goods sector than in the non-traded goods sector tend to have real exchange rate appreciation, which makes their PPP appear to be higher than it really is; and that there should be an adjustment for this "productivity bias." One such adjustment calculated by Goldman Sachs suggests that the dollar was not undervalued in "adjusted-PPP" terms, but was overvalued by some 5-15 percent.

The third approach has been calculated by Swiss Bank Corporation, using FEER, or fundamental equilibrium exchange rate concepts. This calculation also suggests that the dollar was overvalued in the market in early 1998 by as much as 20-30 percent against the DEM and the yen. As noted above, both PPP calculations and FEER calculations can vary on the basis of the assumptions, models, and techniques used.

In recent years, the United States has run substantial current account deficits—a deficit of more than $200 billion is expected in 1998—which might suggest an overvalued dollar. But the fact that those current account deficits have been so easily financed by capital inflows may indicate that the dollar is still considered a bargain at present levels.

(continued on page 112)

(continued from page 111)

Estimates of the U.S. Dollar's Purchasing Power and Fundamental Equilibrium Value

	Market Rate[a] Against the Dollar	PPP Purchasing Power Parity (PPP)		PPP Adjusted for Productivity	Equilibrium Exchange Rate	
		OECD[b]	Penn[c]	Goldman Sachs[d]	IIE	SBC[d]
Deutsche mark	1.77	2.02	2.12	1.51	1.45-1.50	1.40
Japanese yen	132	169	188	124	100	95

[a] On May 11, 1998.
[b] 1997 average.
[c] 1992.
[d] Early 1998.

Sources: Bank for International Settlements Annual Report, 1998, OECD, Penn World Tables 5.6, Goldman Sachs, John Williamson's 1996 informal update of estimates in estimating equilibrium exchange rates, Institute for International Economics (IIE), Washington, D.C. (September 1994) and Swiss Bank Corporation (SBC).

Nevertheless, the portfolio balance approach offers a useful framework for studying exchange rate determination. With its focus on a broad menu of assets, this approach provides richer insights than the monetary approach into the forces influencing exchange rates. It also enables foreign exchange rates to be seen like asset prices in other markets, such as the stock market or bond market, where rates are influenced, not only by current conditions, but to a great extent by market *expectations* of future events. As with other financial assets, exchange rates change continuously as the market receives new information—information about current conditions and information that affects expectations of the future. The random character of these asset price movements does not rule out rational pricing. Indeed, it is persuasively argued that this is the result to be expected in a well-functioning financial market. But in such an environment, exchange rate changes can be large and very difficult to predict, as market participants try to judge the expected real rates of return on their domestic assets in comparison with alternatives in other currencies.

▶ **How Good Are the Various Approaches?**
The approaches noted above are some of the most general and most familiar ones, but there are many others, focusing on differentials in real interest rates, on fiscal policies, and on other elements. The research on this topic has been of great value in enhancing our understanding of long-run exchange rate trends and the issues involved in estimating "equilibrium" rates. It has helped us understand various aspects of exchange rate behavior and particular exchange rate episodes.

Yet none of the available empirical models has proved adequate for making reliable predictions of the course of exchange rates over a period of time. Research thus far has not been able to find stable and significant relationships between exchange rates and any economic fundamentals capable of consistently predicting or explaining short-term rate movements.

2. Foreign Exchange Forecasting In Practice

Most of the approaches to exchange rate determination tell only part of the story—like the several blindfolded men touching different parts of the elephant's body—and other, more comprehensive explanations cannot, in practice, be used for precise forecasting. We do not yet have a way of bringing together all of the factors that help determine the exchange rate in a single comprehensive approach that will provide reliable short- to medium-term predictions.

The exchange rate is a pervasive and complex mechanism, influencing and being influenced by many different forces, with the effects and the relative importance of the different influences continuously changing as conditions change. To the extent that trade flows are a force in the market, competitiveness is obviously important to the exchange rate, and the many factors affecting competitiveness must be considered. To the extent that the money market is a factor, the focus should be on short-term interest rates, and on monetary policy and other factors influencing those short-term interest rates. To the extent that portfolio capital flows matter, the focus should be broadened to include bond market conditions and long-term interest rates. Particularly at times of great international tension, all other factors affecting the dollar exchange rate may be overwhelmed by considerations of "safe haven." Indeed, countless forces influence the exchange rate, and they are subject to continuous and unpredictable changes over time, by a market that is broad and heterogenous in terms of the participants, their interests, and their time frames.

With conditions always changing, the impact of particular events and the response to particular policy actions can vary greatly with the circumstances at the time. Higher interest rates might strengthen a currency or weaken it, by a small amount or by a lot—much depends on *why* the interest rates went up, whether a move was anticipated, what subsequent moves are expected, and the implications for other financial markets, decisions, or government policy moves. Similarly, the results of exchange rate changes are not always predictable: Importers might expect to pay more if their domestic currency depreciates, but not if foreign producers are "pricing to market" in order to establish a beachhead or maintain a market share, or if the importers or exporters had anticipated the rate move and had acted in advance to protect themselves from it.

Nonetheless, those participating in the market must make their forecasts, implicitly and explicitly, day after day, all of the time. Every piece of information that becomes available can be the basis for an adjustment of each participant's viewpoint, or expectations—in other words, a forecast, informal or otherwise. When the screen flashes with an unexpected announcement that, say, Germany has reduced interest rates by a quarter of one percent, that is not just news, it is the basis for countless assessments of the significance of that event, and countless forecasts of its impact in number of basis points.

Those who forecast foreign exchange rates often are divided into those who use "technical" analysis, and those who rely on analysis of "fundamentals," such as GDP, investment, saving, productivity, inflation, balance of payments position, and the like. Technical analysis assumes certain short-term and longer-term patterns in exchange rate movements. It differs from the "random walk" philosophy—the belief that all presently available information has been absorbed into the present exchange rate, and that the next

---

BOX 11-3

ASSESSING FACTORS THAT MAY INFLUENCE EXCHANGE RATES

In the end, it is up to each market participant to decide, in each particular situation, which factors are likely or not likely to move an exchange rate, and what the impact on market expectations will be. It is a matter of judgment; market participants must read the market, decide which data are important, how much weight to give them, and whether and in what way to react—and often these assessments must be made very quickly. Among the considerations to keep in mind in assessing a new piece of information:

1. The Institutional Setting
- Does the currency float, or is it managed—and if so, is it pegged to another currency, basket, or other standard?
- What are its intervention practices? Are they credible, sustainable?

2. Fundamental Analysis
- Does the currency appear overvalued or undervalued in terms of PPP, balance of payments, FEER?
- What is the cyclical situation, in terms of employment, growth, savings, investment, and inflation?
- What are the prospects for government monetary, fiscal, and debt policy?

3. Confidence Factors
- What are market views and expectations with respect to the political environment, and the credibility of the government and central bank?

4. Events
- Are there national or international incidents in the news; possibility of crises or emergencies; governmental or other important meetings coming up?

5. Technical Analysis
- What trends do the charts show? Are there signs of trend reversals?
- At what rates do there appear to be important buy and sell orders? Are they balanced? Is the market over-bought, over-sold?
- What are the thinking and expectations of other market players and analysts?

piece of information as well as the direction of the next rate move is random, with a 50 percent chance the rate will rise, and 50 percent chance it will decline.

Nearly all traders acknowledge their use of technical analysis and charts. According to surveys, a majority say they employ technical analysis to a greater extent than "fundamental" analysis, and that they regard it as more useful than fundamental analysis—a contrast to twenty years ago when most said they relied many more heavily on fundamental analysis. Perhaps traders use technical analysis in part because, at least superficially, it seems simpler, or because the data are more current and timely. Perhaps they use it because traders often have a very short-term time frame and are interested in very short-term moves. They might agree that "fundamentals" determine the course of prices in the long run, but they may not regard that as relevant to their immediate task, particularly since many "fundamental" data become available only with long lags and are often subject to major revisions. Perhaps traders think technical analysis will be effective in part because they know many other market participants are relying on it.

Still, spotting trends is of real importance to traders—"a trend is a friend" is a comment often heard—and technical analysis can add some discipline and sophistication to the process of discovering and following a trend. Technical analysis may add more objectivity to making the difficult decision on when to give up on a position—enabling one to see that a trend has changed or run its course, and it is now time for reconsideration.

Most market participants probably use a combination of both fundamental and technical analysis, with the emphasis on each shifting as conditions change—that is, they form a general view about whether a particular currency is overvalued or undervalued in a structural or longer-term sense, and within that longer-term framework, assess the order flow and all current economic forecasts, news events, political developments, statistical releases, rumors, and changes in sentiment, while also carefully studying the charts and technical analysis.

3. Official Actions To Influence Exchange Rates

As in some other major industrial nations with floating exchange rate regimes, in the United States there is considerable scope for the play of market forces in determining the dollar exchange rate. But also, as in other countries, U.S. authorities do take steps at times to influence the exchange rate, via policy measures and direct intervention in the foreign exchange market to buy or sell foreign currencies. As noted above, in practice, all foreign exchange market intervention of the U.S. authorities is routinely sterilized—that is, the initial effect on U.S. bank reserves is offset by monetary policy action.

No one questions that monetary policy measures can influence the exchange rate by affecting the relative attractiveness of a currency and expectations of its prospects, although it is difficult to find a stable and significant relationship that would yield a predictable, precise response. But the question of the effectiveness of *sterilized* intervention, which has been extensively studied and debated, is much more controversial. Some economists contend that sterilized intervention can have, at best, a modest and temporary effect. Others say it can have a more significant effect by changing expectations about policy and helping to guide the market. Still others believe that the effect depends on the particular market conditions and the intervention strategy of each situation.

Given the present size of U.S. monetary aggregates, balance of payments flows, and the levels of activity in the foreign exchange market and other financial markets, it is widely accepted that any effects of sterilized intervention are likely to be through indirect channels rather than through direct impact on these large aggregates. Empirical tests of sterilized intervention have focused on two main channels through which such intervention might indirectly influence the exchange rate: *the portfolio balance channel and the expectations, or signaling, channel.*

The *portfolio balance channel* postulates that the exchange rate is determined by the balance of supply and demand for available stocks of financial assets held by the private sector. It holds that sterilized intervention will alter the currency composition of assets available to the global private sector, and that if dollar and foreign currency-denominated assets are viewed by investors as imperfect substitutes, sterilized intervention will cause movements in the exchange rate to re-equilibrate supply and demand for dollar assets. The size of this portfolio balance effect would depend on the degree of substitutability between assets denominated in different currencies and on the size of the intervention operation.

The *expectations, or signaling, channel* holds that sterilized intervention may cause private agents to change their expectations of the future path of the exchange rate. Thus, intervention could signal information about the future course of monetary or other economic policies, signal information about, or analysis of, economic fundamentals or market trends, or influence expectations by affecting technical conditions such as bubbles and bandwagons.

A considerable number of studies have found no quantitatively important effects of sterilized intervention through the portfolio balance channel. Some studies have found expectations or signaling effects of varying degrees of significance. Others conclude that the effectiveness depends very much on market conditions and intervention strategy.

There are serious data and econometric problems in studying this question. To assess success, the researcher needs to know the objective of the intervention and other specific details—was the aim to ameliorate a trend, stop a trend, reverse a trend, show a presence, calm a market, discourage speculation, or buy a little time? The researcher also needs to know the counterfactual—what would have happened if the intervention had not taken place. Also, research on this issue must be placed in the broader context of research on exchange rate determination, which, as noted above, indicates that it has not been possible to find stable and significant relationships between exchange rates and any economic fundamentals.

As a practical matter, it is difficult to make sweeping assessments about the success or failure of official intervention operations. Some intervention operations have proven resoundingly successful, while others have been dismal failures. The success or failure of intervention is not so much a matter of statistical probability as it is a matter of how it is used and whether conditions are appropriate. Is the objective reasonable? Does the market look technically responsive? Is intervention anticipated? Will an operation look credible? What is the likely effect on expectations?

In 1983, the Working Group on Foreign Exchange Market Intervention established at the Versailles summit of the Group of Seven warned against expecting too much from official intervention, but concluded that such intervention can be a useful and effective tool in influencing exchange rates in the short run, especially when such operations are consistent with fundamental economic policies. Unquestionably, intervention operations are more likely to succeed when there is a consistency with fundamental economic policies, but it may not always be possible to know whether that consistency exists.

Although attitudes differ, monetary authorities in all of the major countries intervene in the foreign exchange markets at times when they consider it useful or appropriate, and they are likely to continue to do so. The current attitude toward foreign exchange market intervention is summarized in the following excerpt from the June 1996 report of the finance ministers of the Group of Seven nations:

BOX 11-4

CONTINUING CLOSE G7 COOPERATION IN EXCHANGE MARKETS

Exchange rate misalignments can heighten uncertainty in the global economy and can be detrimental to growth and trade. When exchange rates appear to move out of line with underlying fundamentals, close monitoring is necessary and coordinated responses may be required.

We should continue our close cooperation in exchange markets in this foundation, taking into account the fact that:

- A clear and consistent articulation of a common G7 view can have a stabilizing influence and help reinforce the credibility of our commitment to cooperate in the exchange market when circumstances warrant;

- interventions can be effective in certain circumstances, especially when they reinforce changes in policies and/or underlying fundamentals that lead to changes in market expectations about future exchange rates;

- the instrument of intervention must be used judiciously, given its implications for monetary policy and the amount that the authorities can mobilize relative to the size of international capital markets. Nevertheless, these factors do not impede our joint ability to send a clear message to the markets, if and when appropriate;

- interventions are more likely to be effective when they are concerted and reflect a common assessment;

- an important condition for success is the appropriate timing of intervention.

CHAPTER 12

After a generation of revolutionary change in the global foreign exchange market, the question arises, where does that market go from here? What changes can we expect in the future? In some areas, we can point to emerging trends and possible directions

---

1. Global Financial Trends

There is little evidence that the evolution of the world economy toward *deregulation and global integration* is ending, and little reason to expect that the powerful forces that are moving us in those directions will stop suddenly. International trade continues to grow robustly, and international financial transactions and investment far more so. In the United States and many other countries, managed funds are still very heavily invested in domestic assets, which suggests that there is plenty of room for further shifts abroad. Even modest increases in the tendency to look across borders, toward other countries and other currencies for investment opportunities, can have significant implications for levels of activity in the foreign exchange market.

▶ **Introduction of the Euro**
In Europe, the move to a single currency—the *euro*—for participating European Community members is expected to reduce global foreign exchange trading below what it would otherwise be. Indeed, the savings from not having to convert from one member country's currency to another are one of the advantages, or efficiencies, expected from the move to a single currency.

It is very difficult to predict just how much the introduction of the euro will affect the level of foreign exchange turnover. More than half of global foreign exchange trading takes place in EC member countries, but that includes a large amount of currency trading that does not reflect intra-EC transactions. More than half of EC currency trading (or 36 percent of global currency trading) represents foreign exchange trading in the huge international market in London, which transacts foreign exchange business of nations all around the world.

Even so, the move to a single currency could significantly reduce the trend of global turnover in foreign exchange trading. While any estimates can be only approximate, it has been estimated that 10 percent of the global foreign exchange market could disappear with the advent of the euro. This is not a very large decline, against the background of a global market that has been growing by an estimated 13 percent a year in past six years.

The decline is not likely to be spread evenly around European financial centers. Questions have been raised about the continued viability as foreign exchange markets of some of the smaller European trading centers that may feel the brunt of the impact of the move to the euro. There are predictions that Europe's (reduced) levels of currency trading will encourage consolidation into a more limited number of centers.

The euro began having profound effects in currency trading several years before its 1999 introduction date. Market exchange rates for those currencies regarded as almost certain to be among the initial euro participants hardly budged against each other. Beginning in the mid-'90s, those currencies performed as though they were already in a virtually fixed relationship with each other. The trading process among these currencies became cut and dried—not very difficult to carry out, and not very profitable. In those circumstances, advice from market professionals becomes less important and less needed, and market players are less willing to pay for it. Corporations began to do more of their buying and selling on their own. Banks and other dealer institutions cut back considerably on the number of traders— in particular, experienced traders—dealing those currencies.

The introduction of the euro may have other effects quite apart from the impact on overall market turnover. Market observers are considering, among other questions, the euro's possible effects on investment portfolios and on central bank reserve holdings, and its possible use as a vehicle currency and a currency anchor. At present, the dollar's role in the global foreign exchange market and financial system is much larger, relatively speaking, than the U.S. economy's share of world production and trade. (The U.S. accounts for about one-fourth of world production and about one-fifth of international trade, but nearly three-fifths of currency reserves, and the U.S. dollar is one of the two currencies involved in more than four-fifths of foreign exchange transactions). The questions are whether—and if so, in what ways—the euro might assume a major role, and what the implications of any such move would be. To what extent will the euro assume, or share with the dollar, the roles of reserve currency, transactions currency, and investment currency? Will other nations around the world feel more concerned about their rate relationship with the euro than with

the dollar, and shift their intervention focus and their reserves accordingly? Will there be an immediate attraction to the euro, or will the result be, as some market observers expect, official reserves shifting out of EC currencies and into dollars in the near-term, because of the initial uncertainties, then shifting out of dollars and into euros in the longer term as the euro gains in credibility and wider use? It is difficult to forecast these events over an extended period.

If all EC members were to shift to the euro, that would represent an economic group somewhat larger in production and in trade than the United States. Certainly, in that event, it would not be surprising if there were a strong international interest in holding and using the euro, given the economic base and the magnitude of the financial forces behind the new currency, and the interest of others in trade, exchange rate, investment, and other relationships with the EC. But there are many uncertainties, many decisions not yet made, and many events that have not yet occurred that will affect the outcome.

▶ **Increased Trading in Currencies of Emerging Market Countries**

There are estimates that the introduction of the euro may result in a level of global foreign exchange transactions about 10 percent lower than otherwise. However, increasing foreign exchange market activity with respect to some of the *emerging market economies* and *transitional economies* may offset some of the euro's expected dampening impact on turnover. A number of countries in Asia, Eastern Europe, Latin America, and other parts of the world have been growing, opening up their economies, and shifting toward a more international orientation. Their currencies, which are often more volatile and less liquid, and trade with wider spreads than those of the major industrial nations, are playing a more important role in global finance and commerce—and are increasingly traded in exchange markets. Although major problems in Asia and elsewhere have severely affected markets there, many of the emerging markets seem to hold promise of becoming, over time, much more active markets in currency trading. This growth will offset part of the intra-European trading activity that may disappear with the introduction of the euro.

---

2. Shifting Structure Of The Foreign Exchange Market

▶ **Consolidation and Concentration**

After a generation of enormous expansion and integration into a single market, it is reasonable to expect some consolidation and change in the institutional structure of the market.

There is much evidence of consolidation in banking and finance, both in the United States and elsewhere. In the foreign exchange market, with mergers and other forms of restructuring, the number of banks and other firms operating as major dealers and market makers has declined. The number of reporting dealer institutions included in the Federal Reserve surveys declined from 148 to 93 between 1992 and 1998.

Another aspect of consolidation is reflected in the steps taken by many major players to cut back on the number of their outlets, the number of financial centers around the world where they actively trade foreign exchange. The business of trading currencies is highly competitive and pressures are particularly severe during periods of less volatile rates and less rapid growth in turnover. With pressure on profit margins, and with expanding technology increasing the costs of outfitting and operating trading rooms, institutions search for ways to improve efficiency. They look for ways to operate in fewer centers— with fewer traders, fewer trading desks, and less of the expensive equipment that trading desks require—without losing business. With improved technology and strong emphasis on marketing, some feel that they can service their customers and meet their own proprietary trading needs more efficiently and more competitively with fewer outlets. Some are consolidating to the extent that they limit themselves to a single trading center in each of the three major time zones, while others take different approaches. The tendency toward market concentration has been evident in smaller markets, which some non-local banks have been abandoning, and also in the largest centers. We have seen some increase in the market share of the largest dealers in a number of major centers. In both the U.S. and U.K. markets, the ten largest institutions account for half of total transactions, Whether a trend toward concentration will continue will be influenced by many factors, including technology—for example, the prospects for increased use of the internet in foreign exchange trading, and further development of automated order-matching.

▶ **Automated Order-Matching Systems**

As technology continues to progress, it doubtlessly will further transform the foreign exchange trading process, and lead to new concepts and new technology. Of great interest is the advance of electronic brokerage systems— computer facilities that match orders among participating dealer institutions around the world. These systems (as noted in Chapter 7) have had a major and growing impact since their introduction in 1992. The share of total foreign exchange trading handled by electronic brokering is 13 percent of total turnover in the United States, and 11 percent in London, and it continues to grow. More significant is the much larger and rapidly growing share of turnover in those segments of the market where electronic brokering is most popular—that is, spot transactions in a limited number of high volume currency pairs (such as dollar-mark) where there is much liquidity and a heavy flow of trading activity. In such markets, automated order-matching systems can offer very tight spreads of one or two basis points, or about one-third of previous spreads.

The two electronic brokers presently operating (Reuters and Electronic Broking Service, or EBS) have gained an important market share, and have attracted business from voice brokers and also from banks dealing directly with each other by telephone and other channels. Brokers and others adversely affected by this development are, understandably, seeking to respond by improving their own practices, broadening the services they provide, and making their operations more efficient.

Electronic brokering initially concentrated on the spot market for the most popular currency pairs, but it is moving into other segments of the market. There are now some transactions in the forward market, and interest rate products are being developed. It is expected that in the future more market participants will be arranging their foreign exchange transactions directly with counterparties, rather than feeding the transactions up through major dealers and voice brokers. Looking ahead, certainly the further development of electronic broking could have important implications for future market liquidity and mode of operation.

---

3. New Instruments, New Systems

The development of derivative instruments continues. Non-deliverable forwards and options are being used in some emerging markets. Building on that concept, some market participants see a significant future role for "foreign exchange, difference settled" (FXDS) more broadly. The instrument would be used for key currencies and for spot as well as forward trades, for transactions where the counterparties do not want delivery of the underlying currencies, and arrange to settle by paying or receiving only the difference between their contract price and a benchmark exchange rate. However, various operational issues—and, in the United States, also regulatory issues—remain to be resolved.

One effect of FXDS would be a reduction in settlements and settlement risks. This might complement the effort initiated by a consortium of international banks to create a bank, CLS bank, which would carry out continuous linked settlements of foreign exchange transactions, so that one bank's money would be paid over only simultaneously with its counterparty's payment.

To conclude, looking to the future, to a large extent, the shape and direction of the foreign exchange market will depend, not only on these technical issues, but also on how nations and governments of the world manage their affairs. Can we look to a period of good economic policy and progress, with markets reasonably stable and effective, or will there be large-scale disruptions and volatility of the kind we have experienced at times in the past? The foreign exchange market will adapt to the circumstances within which it is obliged to operate and respond to changing conditions in the world economy and financial environment.

FOOTNOTES

▶ 1 Estimates of dealer turnover in "non-traditional" OTC products and in exchange-traded products are not reported in the same way as the "traditional" OTC products, and it is difficult to compare the two in a meaningful way

▶ 2 IMF *International Capital Markets*, September 1996 Washington, D C , p 122

▶ 3 As noted in Chapter 8, one of the approaches being explored for dealing with "settlement risk"—the risk that one bank pays out currency to settle a trade, but the counterparty bank does not pay out the other currency—is *netting +*, a technique for rolling settlement forward from day to day by using tom-next swaps

▶ 4 Bank for International Settlements, *66th Annual Report*, June 1996, p 160

▶ 5 For example, on July 1, two netting + counterparties determine that on July 2, Party A owes CHF 300 million (Swiss francs) to Party B, and B owes $200 million to A Under netting +, a tom-next swap would be executed under which A buys CHF 300 million from B for value July 2 and sells CHF 300 million to B for value July 3, at current market rates The CHF cash flows for July 2 are thus netted down to zero (no CHF delivery) and the residual U S dollar cash flow remains to be paid by one party to the other (Thus, if the July 2 leg of the tom-next swap was done at $1 = CHF 1 5152, i e for $198 million, B would pay A $2 million) Payments related to the "next" part of the tom-next swap would be combined with other cash flows due July 3, which, in turn, would be offset by a new tom-next swap, and so on (New York Foreign Exchange Committee, *Guidelines for Foreign Exchange Settlement Netting*)

▶ 6 For a discussion of fundamental and technical models of exchange rate determination, see Rosenberg, M R , *Currency Forecasting*, Irwin, 1996.

▶ 7 IMF, Washington D C, 1998 "Exchange Rate Assessment: Extensions of the Macroeconomic Balance Approach" Occasional Paper 167 Edited by Peter Isard and Hamid Faruqee

▶ 8 Bank for International Settlements, *68th Annual Report*, June 1998, pp. 103-105

CPSIA information can be obtained at www.ICGtesting.com
Printed in the USA
BVOW11s2104070715

407804BV00003B/64/P